A Year in Ink

VOLUME 2

A Year in Ink

SAN DIEGO WRITERS, INK

ANTHOLOGY

VOLUME 2

Edited by Sandra Alcosser and Arthur Salm

THE
INK SPOT
PRESS

San Diego, California

A Year in Ink is a publication of
Ink Spot Press
San Diego Writers, Ink
PO Box 34374
San Diego, CA 92163

Editorial coordinators: Victoria Melekian
                         Judy Reeves

Copy Editor: Donna Marganella

Cover art: Railway Bridge near Heidelberg, Germany, 1981
          ©1981 Philipp Scholz Rittermann

Design and typography: Armadillo Creative

ISBN 978-0-9799204-2-4

Printed in the United States of America
Printed by Lightning Source Inc.

CONTENTS

Introduction . . . . .Sandra Alcosser 1

Introduction . . . . .Arthur Salm 2

National Anthem .Ilya Kaminsky. 5

Stolen Memories .D.B. (Donna) Cunningham . . .6

Four Men . . . . .Steve Kowit 13

Bread and Onions . . . . .Deniz Perin. 14

Three Out of My Five Children . . . . .Peter Hepburn. 15

Room 78 . . . . .Christine Rikkers. 18

Last Day in Wuhan . . . . .Dolores Young. 19

Terra Incognita. .Kimberly Schultz. 20

Mother of Pearl .Carolyn Selman. 27

Conversation About the Moon . . . . .Eric Johnson 28

Small Favors . . . . .Judy Hamilton 29

On The Edge. . . . . .Roger Aplon. 35

74,500 People Die in an Earthquake . . . .Pallie Wells. 36

Baby, It's You . . . . .Judy Geraci 37

Breaking the Weather. . . . . .Lizzie Wann 45

Rain. . . . . .Margo Wilding. 46

Cecil . . . . .Sandra Joss 47

History . . . . .Crystal Hadidian 51

San Diego at 1 a.m. . . . . .Meagan Marshall. 52

Boom Dreams. . . . . .Stephen W. Potts 53

Full of Grace . . . . .Lenny Lianne 61

Listeners as the Photo is Taken. . . . . . . .Kathleen Elliott Gilroy 62

Passing. . . . . .Steve Montgomery. 63

My Tulips' Interment . . . . .Sydney Brown 71

At Aqbat Jaber . . . . .Chris Baron 72

One of These Nights . . . . .Steve Montgomery 73

old guy . . . . .Gary Winters 81

Ars Poetica . . . . .Una Nichols Hynum 82

Just Passing Through . . . . .Dave Riessen 83

sunflower . . . . .Michael Rancourt 94

The Rush . . . . .Veronica Andrew 95

The Moon Daughter . . . . .Zoe Ghahremani 96

Line Dancing at The Cadillac . . . . .Lisa Hemminger 104

This Bird Chest Holds a Bird . . . . .David Tomas Martinez 105

Elevator Music . . . . .Erik Kiviat 106

I Am Shomer . . . . .Allison Wright 113

My Father's Gift . . . . .Stephen McDonald 114

Riding an Indian . . . . .J. F. MacDonald 115

Curtain—An Elegy . . . . .Sylvia Levinson 117

Erin in black stockings . . . . .Billy Hughes 118

Remembering the '80s . . . . .Eber Lambert 119

Palinode . . . . .Brian Hayter 123

Uzurazuki (The Month of Quail) . . . . . . .Jeannine Hall Gailey 124

On Seeing Peter for the Last Time . . . . .Josie Gable Rodriguez 125

Guidelines . . . . .Billie Dee 127

Contributors 129

Introduction

A n anthology begins in the earth and in the mind—*anthos*, a slender stalk of pollen, meets *logos*, the word made flesh.

From thorn mint to button celery, from willow flycatcher to fairy shrimp, from three million acres of dry and fragrant hillsides and ephemeral vernal pools these words arise, and from almost four hundred poems we selected thirty to move in couplets between stories.

Philipp Scholz Ritterman's cover photograph initiates our invitation. Born in Lima, Peru, he became a photographer in Europe, and now lives in San Diego County. While his images illuminate uncelebrated subjects, they reside in the collections of the Museum of Modern Art and Bibliotheque Nationale de Paris.

San Diego is a landscape of humble and sublime beauty compressed under thousands of miles of pavement. These words and images, created in the most diverse county in America, with the greatest number of native species at risk, celebrate the radiant symmetries that join us. As contemporary American poet Galway Kinnell wrote—*sometimes it is necessary to reteach a thing its loveliness*—and so we offer gratitude to San Diego and San Diego Writers, Ink for graciously inviting our stories and poems.

Sandra Alcosser
November 2008

Introduction

One of the best, and worst parts of my almost-20-year job as Books editor of the *San Diego Union-Tribune* was interviewing writers. Best, because I got to talk at length with the likes of (assume a series of impressive big-time hotshot names here). Worst, because not infrequently I'd find myself talking to someone who quite simply did not want to be talking to me. His or her talent lay in writing, not in explaining his or her art to a stranger who was either scribbling in a notebook, if the interview was in person, or producing ominous background keyboardy clacks over the phone.

Sometimes, trying to loosen the conversation up a bit, I'd ask an author to describe a typical day at work. The responses were all over the clock: morning, afternoon, night. And all through the wardrobe: pajamas, beach attire, business casual. (No nakeds. None owned up to, anyway.) Likewise the process of putting a book together—everything from "I have to know the ending before I start"/"I write the last page first" to "I have no idea what's going to happen"/"The characters keep surprising me." Longhand, typewriter, computer; detailed outline, rough outline, no outline; 3 x 5 index cards, 4 x 6 index cards, "Index cards? Why would I use index cards?"

But I had no names, much less voices or faces, to latch onto as I read through the submissions for this second Year in Ink, and maybe it was this blind selection process that jump-started what became my fantastical musings about the writers. I imagined "The Moon Daughter" being written between diaper changes. "Small Favors," I hoped, wasn't cathartic, while "Terra Incognito," an equally harrowing tale, couldn't possibly have been—it's too much fun. "Elevator Music" was angry enough and funny enough to summon an image of Steve Allen reading aloud Letters to the Editor in the furious, indignant spirit in which they were written. If "Three Out of My Five Children" doesn't exist as a spoken-word/stand-up performance, it should; try to read it without seeing the puzzled-looking author on a tiny stage, fiddling with the mic stand, blocked occasionally by a waitress delivering watered-down drinks to a table of louts. (They don't get the routine, but you do, which makes it even funnier.)

There is no unifying theme to these pieces—nor should there be. After all, my category is prose, and the collection includes nonfiction, memoir, short story, excerpts from novels. Well, you might detect a similarity between two of the memoir excerpts, "Passing" and "One of These Nights," because they're from the same memoir. They're both in here because they're both that good.

Some of the pieces are set in the San Diego area, some seem as if they might be, some aren't; in the selection process, geography was not a criterion. And as much as I'd like to add a "but" here, and go on to cobble together something about a certain only-in-San-Diego ethos that a discerning reader will be able to detect in all the pieces, I can't, because there isn't. These are writers, after all: pajamas, beach attire, business casual. There may be waves breaking outside the window, ashes from the latest firestorm may have drifted into the keyboard, but at one point you're still going to find yourself at Idaho State University in 1978.

I confess to being a contrarian, San Diego Writers, Ink-wise, when it comes to the idea of writers as a literal, physical community. Maybe it comes from working in a newsroom for so many years, where you can't fire off a shotgun without winging half a dozen good writers; for all the camaraderie, one pretty much has to adopt a secret my-work's-important,-I'm-busy,-who-the-hell-cares-about-yours? attitude.

But a figurative, literary community? Oh, yes, indeed. Although I find suspect all references to mysterious forces that cannot be detected by a scientific instrument—preferably one that produces sine waves and makes spacey, neat-o sounds—it's impossible to ignore the feeling that San Diego is approaching a critical artistic mass, one that could result in a stunning literary explosion. A chain reaction may have already begun. Consider this volume a sample of core material.

Arthur Salm
October 2008

National Anthem

Ilya Kaminsky

"You must speak not only of great devastation
but of two women kissing in the yellow grass!"

I heard this not from a great philosopher
but from my brother Tony

who could do four haircuts in thirteen minutes,
his eyes closed. Recited our National Anthem in the
     mirror with his eyes closed.

"You must drink cucumber vodka and naked sing
     all night.
Unite women and boys of the Earth!"

He played the accordion out of tune in a country
where the only musical instrument is the door.

"Speak not only of great devastation."
so said my brother, who could not write or read

but spent his days covered in other people's hair.

Stolen Memories

D.B. (Donna) Cunningham

(For Tillie Smith)

I was afraid the goats would smother back in the U-Haul. The goats weren't very big. The U-Haul was one of those covered orange trailers, and I wondered how Marcy would explain the smell when we took it back to the rental place. I suggested an open trailer, but Marcy predicted there would be goat meat all over I-5 if we tried the trip with an open trailer, so we hitched the smallest, cheapest covered trailer we could rent to the back of my '64 Lincoln. The car had about 180,000 miles on it. I trusted it to take us to Stockton and back in well-worn comfort. I kept my fingers crossed that the car would survive the trip.

Getting rid of the goats was a good idea. Marcy's 86-year-old grandmother had given her one goat as a present, saying mysteriously that the goat would bring Marcy home. I thought a goat was a strange gift to give someone who loved Led Zeppelin, but Marcy's grandmother was a gypsy, so maybe goat-giving was a family tradition. The goat was a cute animal, about the size of a dog . . . at first. The goat lived on Marcy's porch with the washer and dryer, and careened around the living room. Marcy liked to walk the goat on a leash. People approached her carefully to ask what breed of dog it was. Marcy patiently explained that it was an African pygmy goat.

After a few months the goat was less cute. It had grown gnarly corkscrew horns and was mean. Marcy moved it from its home in the laundry room to her front yard, where it butted the metal mesh of the fence with such ferocity that the mailman refused to deliver the mail.

Marcy got a female Nubian goat because she thought the male pygmy would calm down if he had some company. The Nubian got pregnant, the Billy was meaner than ever, and before long Marcy had three pet goats. Her neighbors were annoyed by the small herd roaming her suburban yard, and Marcy was spending a lot of money on goat chow. She advertised the goats for sale in the newspaper and managed to sell the kid. No one wanted the mean pygmy and the Nubian both, and Marcy wouldn't split the couple up, seeing them somehow as a metaphor for modern relationships.

Marcy's grandmother, Tillie, suggested a solution—take the goats to Uncle Jess, who lived on a farm in Jenny Lind, California. He could offer the goats the wide-open spaces they needed and deserved. As long as we were driving north, she reasoned, we might as well take Tillie along. She wanted to visit her sister. They hadn't seen each other in five years, and although they never liked each other, Tillie was 86 and Misella was 80. The time for a reunion had come.

I knew Marcy's family well. We spent a lot of time together. Tillie came to stay with Marcy for long periods of time and she told good stories and cooked pea soup. Marcy's family looked normal on the surface. Her father was a stern authoritarian, but he lost control early. Marcy had gotten pregnant, married, and divorced while still in high school. Her two daughters had two different fathers. At 28, Marcy was planning her third marriage, and longing for more kids. The secret of Marcy's family was that it was an absolute matriarchy. The women made up the rules. They were tall, blond, and strong-willed and they were gypsies, descended from the gypsies of the British Isles.

Five of us left in the Lincoln at sunset: Marcy, the two pre-teen daughters with different fathers, her grandmother, and me. And the goats in the U-Haul.

Grandma Tillie was on a mission that had been brewing for five years. There were family keepsakes at Aunt Misella's house, and Tillie wanted them. The family had traveled around the American West in covered wagons, selling lace and telling fortunes. Gypsies traveled light, so wealth was measured in quality, not quantity. There was silver, fine linen and antique jewelry in the family, but Marcy's grandmother didn't want these valuables. She was after old photographs. The pictures she wanted most were of her and Willie, the second cousin she was supposed to marry, only to have him die of appendicitis on their wedding day. These pictures, along with Willie's spurs, were taken by Aunt Misella during a busy family reunion. No one used the word "steal."

"Gypsies don't steal!" Marcy's grandmother stated. She was the only gypsy I had ever met, and if she said gypsies didn't steal, I was prepared to believe her. Stealing or not, somehow Tillie's younger sister ended up with the family pictures. Since Tillie was oldest at 86, she felt the pictures were rightfully hers.

We drove up the Grapevine, the highway that went over the mountains into California's central valley. Marcy's kids were well-behaved and snuggled in the back seat under the quilts. Marcy's grandmother sat in a corner of the back seat watching warily out of the window. As I drove, she recounted how the land we were passing had once been planted with cotton. She marveled at how fast the Lincoln covered the miles compared to the horse and wagon. She said she missed the slower days of the past, where she could almost get to know people before the family picked up and moved on.

We pulled off at a truck stop coffee shop where Tillie leered suspiciously at a young highway patrolman. "*Muskra*. Never trust them," she whispered.

"*Muskra* is the gypsy word for cop. Grandma Tillie hates cops," Marcy explained.

As we drove, the darkness was pierced occasionally by a train headlight. Tillie described how she had crossed Death Valley mostly on foot, to spare the horses in the hot weather.

"Then we got to San Bernardino," Tillie said with a sigh. Tillie described San Bernardino as if it were some beautiful mystical oasis, not the diesel-fumed truck stop it had become. "The first green we saw in two weeks was those orange trees," she mused. "And we could smell their perfume long before we saw them."

"When you traveled, how did you make money?" I asked.

"The men shoed horses and sharpened knives," she explained. "And the women went calling."

"You mean visiting?" I asked.

"We called on people," she said. "We knocked on their doors and showed them some pretty lace for sale. But the lace was just to get us in the door," she confided. "Once inside, we *dukkered*."

"Told fortunes," Marcy translated.

"Can you really see into the future?" I asked.

"Don't need to," Tillie answered. "You can tell a lot about people just by really looking at them—their faces, how worn their hands are, what pictures they have on their walls, what books. I always said, 'You will receive a letter.' That's a good one. Everyone receives a letter sooner or later. But mainly you just tell people what you think they want to hear. We made a lot of money that way."

The plan was to leave Marcy's kids and grandmother at Aunt Misella's house, then proceed to Jenny Lind to drop off the goats. Misella's porch light was on. Aunt Misella opened the door. She was an old lady with a round, pleasant face. She wore fluffy slippers, a pink chenille bathrobe, and a hairnet. A three-legged dog in a plaid jacket hobbled to the door, excited to see us. We ushered Marcy's sleepy children into the bedroom and left the two old sisters to drink tea and talk. They greeted each other warily, but seemed to warm up as they put the kettle on.

"The dog only has three legs," I commented when we were back in the car. Marcy shrugged it off like it was normal. I guess it was, compared to keeping goats as house pets. Marcy tried hard to remember how to get to Jenny Lind. After two more hours of driving through blackness, we turned onto an uphill dirt road. I was dead tired, but Marcy urged me on.

"What if we were gypsies, traveling like Tillie and Misella, across the desert. Would you just give up?" she challenged. "The house must be at the end of this road."

I imagined myself a skeleton in the Mojave. I imagined myself a skeleton in Jenny Lind. It was awfully quiet in the U-Haul. I wondered if the goats were dead. The road narrowed. The Lincoln was a wide car and I began to worry about getting stuck. Finally, Marcy said "You'd better stop. There's a cliff on my side, and we're close to the edge."

The headlights illuminated a road that seemed to melt into the brush. "Better back up," Marcy suggested. I had never really learned to drive a car with a trailer hooked up to it. As long as I was going forward, I was OK, but when it came to backing up, I was lost. I didn't remember if I should turn the wheel in the same direction I wanted the trailer to go in, or the opposite direction—it was one of those confusions like remembering whether you were supposed to starve a fever and feed a cold or the other way around. The trailer seemed to sway from side to side with a will of its own. I switched off the ignition, accepting my own inadequacy.

"I'm waiting until it's light," I declared. "It's four a.m. and we're nowhere near a desert. I need to do this when it's light." Marcy reluctantly agreed. I stretched out on the front seat and Marcy stretched out on the back seat and we slept until dawn.

Stopping had been a good idea. In the daylight we could see that we had turned off on the wrong dirt road. I backed slowly down the road. The goats kicked around in the trailer. Marcy's uncle wasn't surprised to see us when we arrived at 6:30 AM. He made us breakfast and took the goats out of the trailer and put them in a field where they cavorted happily. He even swept out the U-Haul. Marcy bid the goats an emotional farewell. They responded by munching grass. The empty U-Haul clattered along behind us on the way back to Stockton. We returned it and arrived at Misella's house ready for lunch.

Aunt Misella's furniture was dark green Naugahyde. A round woven rug covered the polished wooden floor. In the kitchen we sat on green vinyl chairs around a metal kitchen table with a gray marbled linoleum top, and the most ornate silver tea service I had ever seen. Tillie served us tea and tuna sandwiches. Marcy's grandmother was a wonderful cook. Her pea soup was the best I'd ever eaten. Her stews and soups were always seasoned with fresh herbs. She introduced me to greens and to turnips, with stern instructions never to pick the greens at the edge of the field, only the ones from the middle, where no animals or men were likely to pee. She tried to teach Marcy and me to cook like her, but our cooking never tasted as good, probably because we bought our vegetables at the market.

When Misella left the room, Tillie turned from sweet old lady to shrewd conspirator. "Here's the plan," she hissed to us. "We'll take the children to a barbeque. You stay here and when we're gone, you go into Misella's bedroom closet and find the box with the pictures and take it. Put everything back where you found it, and she won't know for years that I took them."

I had never stolen anything in my life. Nothing. I was so afraid of getting in trouble that I wouldn't even consider pocketing a pack of gum. Marcy, on the other had a more liberal point of view. Marcy had been arrested once, on the unlikely felony charge of horse stealing. She had saved an abused horse and its owner filed charges. They were later dropped when Marcy proved that the horse was mistreated. I was appalled at Marcy's Robin Hood attitude toward the law, but I recognized her higher morality. Maybe it was gypsy morality. I also admired her courage. I was not so brave and here I was, an accessory, not even a gypsy, and plotting a theft from a house not owned by anyone related to me.

Aunt Misella and Grandma Tillie took the kids to the barbeque; Tillie whispered some last-minute instructions, "Remember to put everything back where you found it."

The silence in the house was broken only by the sound of the three-legged dog's toenails clicking on the hardwood floor. In Misella's bedroom, a dresser had been moved in front of the closet door. I helped Marcy move it away, realizing I was leaving fingerprints all over everything and wishing I had brought gloves.

"This is it," Marcy whispered, although there was no one else was in the house. "You stand by the door and make sure no one comes in. I'll find the box." Marcy opened the closet door and we were confronted with a Chinese puzzle of boxes: department store boxes, shoe boxes, cigar boxes, and cardboard cartons stacked floor to ceiling, filling every available inch of the closet.

"We've got to remember how these are stacked up, so we can put them back the way they were," Marcy said. She took boxes down one at a time, glanced at their contents, and piled them in the middle of the bedroom. We went through layers of Misella's past like we were on an archeological dig. We found chiffon scarves from the sixties, polka-dotted material from the fifties, and hats with veils from the forties. Near the bottom of the stack was a cardboard carton. Marcy opened it.

"This is it!" she exclaimed. I wanted to look, but she wouldn't let me. "Not here," she hissed. "We don't want to get caught."

I helped her stack the boxes back up in the closet, rebuilding the layers the way we had found them. We moved the dresser back in front of the closet door. We carried the box out to the Lincoln and put it in the trunk.

"Go!" Marcy commanded. Adrenaline pumping, I drove the getaway car. We parked about six blocks away under a pepper tree with long drooping branches that shielded us from the traffic. We opened the box.

There were riches in memories: A tintype of Marcy's great-grandmother when she was young. Photos of Tillie and Misella as little girls, staring wide-eyed at the camera. A picture of a family standing around a campfire that eerily included a three-legged dog. A group of people standing in front of a tent under a banner that read "Buy Our Elixir." At the bottom of the box were metal spurs. "Willie's spurs," Marcy whispered, like we were looking at emeralds.

Tillie, Misella, and the kids returned from the barbeque. Marcy's grandmother was in a hurry to get on the road. She told Misella that I didn't drive too well after dark. She pecked her sister on the cheek goodbye, and we headed south. Before we got on the freeway, we pulled over and presented Tillie with the box from the trunk. She squinted at the photos in the twilight, and when she found the spurs she cried. We had stolen back her memories, she said. As we drove, she explained who all the people in the pictures were, and sang us songs from her girlhood until we reached home.

Four Men

Steve Kowit

Four men in hooded sweatshirts
jump from the brush & tear across
the road at Dogpatch, Rural 94,
right in front of my Ford Ranger
which, it's such a winding road,
they couldn't see coming. I brake
to let the last one pass,
their backpacks heavy, one
would guess, with jugs of water.
High desert. Dead of summer.
Out here, the Border Patrol
cruises night & day, so it isn't
bloody likely they'll get thru.
Long ago, we stole this half
of what was Mexico. After
Whitman saw the snow on a spree
with the northwest wind
he said: "It put me out of conceit
of fences & imaginary lines."
They dash across the road. Not
the first time that I've said
it could be anywhere: Palestine,
Afghanistan, Iraq. Illegals.
Desperate to find work. Under
my breath, but fervently, I wish
them luck. Four men at Dogpatch,
Rural 94, have raced across the road
& disappeared into the trees & brush.

Bread and Onions

Deniz Perin

We tread the basaltic wall of Diyarbakir. On the ground, sunflower seed shells, dust. Behind the wall, shanty homes. Watermelons grow, unstoppable, on the banks of the Tigris. *Amed*, Nuhat tells me, *is the real name of this town*. Two children throw rocks. A woman, middle-aged, walks by with grocery bags. In the bags, bread and onions. Nuhat stops, speaks to her in Kurdish. *What do you think*, he asks, *will they ever let us be?* We glance at the tank rolling by, cannon pointed out. She does not answer. Only smiles wistfully, reaches into her bag, offers us a loaf of bread.

Three Out of My Five Children

Peter Hepburn

Frank has always been the most trouble. He's my first son by my second wife. Her name is Dolly and she is a piece of work. Frank has always taken the attitude that I don't love him. Even when he was a boy and I was living with my third wife and he was living with Dolly and the other boy, he'd say things like, "You don't love me." I'd say things back to him like, "You can't know that for sure." I was just ribbing him of course. He knew how I really felt.

Katie is my pride and joy. Her nickname is Blanche. Katie has decided to be an actress. I don't know why she has that nickname. It's not because of Blanche Dubois from the Tennessee Williams play. Bunny, her mother, has called her Blanche since the delivery room. I don't know where the acting bug comes from either. She doesn't get that from my side of the family. We don't believe in emotional displays.

Bunny was wife number one and the biggest piece of work I'd ever known until I met Dolly. Every time I get married it feels like my feet have just landed on a floor covered in marbles and nails. Katie is a real beauty and that's more than I can say for Bunny. I include myself in Bunny's ugly category so don't make it sound like I'm anti-woman or whatever. I only mention it because I love Katie very much even though she's nothing like me. She inherited her beauty from somewhere and it isn't from me or Bunny. Maybe true beauty skips a generation but I tried looking back across my family tree and have come up empty. The same is true about Bunny's kin where things get even more repulsive with all the cousins marrying each other and everything. There isn't a good-looking grandparent, uncle, aunt, or cousin to be found in either one of our shaky trees. Katie is noticed at every family gathering is all I'm saying.

I met Bunny in the same bar where I met my third and fourth wives. Blanchard's is a dive bar and mostly ugly people drink there. Bunny threw my bowling ball out the window of our apartment only two weeks after we were married. We lived on the fourth floor of an apartment on a busy street. If you're curious about what a bowling ball and a sidewalk look like after a bowling ball hits from four stories up then either throw one out and watch or just marry Bunny and try belonging to four bowling leagues. If you don't want to exercise either of those options then take my word for it that when a bowling ball and a sidewalk collide the two look about as good as Bunny. After the divorce Bunny told me, and I quote, "You're the worst lover I've ever had and that includes both of your brothers." She'll say anything to get my goat.

A few months ago I bumped into Ronald Grundy. He was Bunny's husband just before me and just after Lou Kadidis. Ron told me that when he found out Bunny was cheating on him he really wasn't that upset.

"Why weren't you angry?" I said.

"She was such a good cook and she seemed kind of happy," he said.

Frankly, I think Ron wanted to be mad but he's about a foot shorter and sixty pounds lighter than me. Who knows? Maybe he is a saint? After all, he married Bunny. Ron mentioned at the very end of our brief chat that he and Bunny were cheating on Lou.

"I was putting the pork to Bunny before and after her marriage to Lou. I knew what was in store for me when I married her," he said.

"I'm glad she was faithful to me," I said.

Ron gave me a funny look that I took to mean he was kind of jealous of my bedroom talents. He excused himself right after that.

Katie sent me a poem on my last birthday. It came about three months late and there wasn't a card but still, she sent me a poem. Here is what it said:

> *I know it's not your birthday.*
> *I know that you're my dad.*
> *This is just my way of saying,*
> *You're the father I never had.*

I never have been much at reading poetry or books or magazines or newspapers, but isn't that wonderful? She sends me birthday cards every three or four years and there's always a poem even though she forgets the card. She keeps forgetting to send me her phone number but she's an actress and I suppose that's the kind of thing actresses do.

Douglas is the gay one. He's the oldest and I love him just as much as my regular children. I never use the F word anymore when he's around. I even believe that the gays should be allowed to marry. I told Douglas, who hates it when people call him Doug, that he should get into designing or whatever. He's an insurance investigator so I guess you never know. Doug moved away to college and didn't come home until the year after his mom and I got divorced. I heard that he came home on weekends a lot right after I moved across the river. Maybe he didn't like the way my wife always yelled at me about drinking and staying out late. She should have been more sensitive in front of him. I met a few of Doug's friends outside the bowling alley a few months ago. I mentioned to them that his voicemail must have not been working because he doesn't return my calls. They just looked at me funny and said they were in a hurry. When they got a few feet away, I'm pretty sure I overheard one of them call the other one a creep.

Well, that's three of the five children. One of the other two is kind of mad at me over the whole child support issue and I'm not sure what is troubling that other boy. I've been meaning to send them a few bucks but my current wife thinks she might be pregnant. I'm heading over to Blanchard's if you want to join me. The bartender's name is Whitey. He's the handsomest barkeep I've ever seen. Every time he brings me a drink he gives me a funny look. For some reason he always puts me in a foul mood.

Room 78, St. Francis Memorial Hospital

Christine Rikkers

There is a church in my stomach.
The people come and go—
they pray, they weep, they
sing. The roof was constructed
when I was eight years old,
the rest stone by stone
as I grew. I have never seen
the inside, but I am told it is
luminous. It was built a mere
three centimeters from my liver.
I imagine a dome
the texture of orange peel,
and inside pews of almond
with inlay of opal.
In bed, hidden in the licorice
breath of poppies, I pray
the church still stands.
The women tell me it must be
destroyed—there is not
enough room in my stomach.
Around my face their hands flap
and flutter, smell of silver.
Attendance at my church
has grown too quickly
forcing countless new churches
to spring up in my bones. But each time
I pass a mirror, I am surprised
I am not a bit shrunken—
I am sixty-four and full
of peace. They tell me this.
They come and go.

Last Day In Wuhan

Dolores Young

The pedicab driver sobs at the roadside,
his vehicle blistered by an army truck,
no money to fix it.

A long line outside the bank,
anxious to cash out accounts
before government takes all.

The radio wails
the latest hit,
"After I married you
my luck ran out . . . "

A kiosk mobbed by students.
They merely browse,
thirsty for the latest news.

When will they come?
Any time. Better get out now.

The outstretched hand
of the food vendor.
I try to pay,
but the crowded train jolts
and I miss her.
She stands at the station with her hand empty.

"Sorry, sorry."
My voice trembles,
as the train pulls away.

The conductor intones,
Little Eastern Gate Station.

Out of the window I see
my school in night's darkness.
Stars still twinkle
above the dormitory roof,
my friends asleep in their beds,

not knowing I am leaving,
not knowing I am weeping.

Terra Incognita

Kimberly Schultz

I'm surprised we haven't been threatened at gunpoint before. Of course, the wackadoo showed up on Liz's day off, so my customer service skills must save my life. This was not covered in training four months ago.

"Sir, I can see that you're upset," I say, obeying the first rule of customer service: recognize the customer's concerns. I stay seated behind my desk and keep my hands in the air. There's no panic button for me to press anyway; we're not a bank.

"I am beyond fucking upset," the man says, and his gun weaves from side to side. I don't know guns, but I recognize the *sh-shunk* noise of a shotgun being loaded. Even a convenience store would have a silent alarm button. I am completely fucked.

"Yes, sir," I say. Rule two: the customer is always right. I take a deep breath to calm myself like we do in yoga, but it's hard with a gun pointed at me. His eyes are gray like a mouse or squirrel, some rodent. They won't stop moving. His gaze travels all over the room, to the door beside my desk, to Liz's empty office, to the three faded purple armchairs that make up our waiting area.

He's waiting. He didn't have a plan, that much is evident. At least he should have worn gloves. He's left fingerprints on the doorknobs, the jamb of the office supply closet, and all the papers on Liz's desk.

I have no idea what to say. My friend from junior college works for the Department of Defense. She had hostage training. They told her to be as bland and anonymous as possible until they start shooting people. Then she should get the hell out of there. It's hard to be anonymous when it's only you.

"I want to see the fucking records," he says.

"Of course, sir," I say without thinking. "Files are in that cabinet over there." I jerk my right hand in the direction of the lateral file.

"Don't move," he says, then reconsiders. "No, get up. Get up and lie down over there." He motions with the shotgun to the center of the room, the rug Liz bought on clearance at Pier 1.

I get up from my chair, trip over the legs, and catch myself on the edge of my desk. He jumps, but doesn't pull the trigger.

"Sorry," I say. I really don't want to be shot at all, but I don't want to be shot for clumsiness.

"Just move," he says. When I stand, I see that he is not much taller than me. Without the mass of curly hair holding up his Dodgers cap, we might be the same height. "Face down, hands on your head."

I kneel and then lower myself to the carpet with both hands. I don't want to look threatening; I don't want to look enticing. Too anxious to make sure my weight is balanced, I put my face on the scratchy carpet and place one hand next to my ear, one on the back of my neck. I inhale rubber fumes from the carpet backing when I try another yoga breath.

I watch him walk to the file cabinet. He hefts the gun to his left hand so his right is free.

He rattles the drawer. I hear the dull, unyielding thud. Oh, hell.

Rule three: Solve the customer's problem as if it were your own, because it is.

"Top drawer," I say to the carpet.

"What?" he says. I prop myself up on one elbow to be heard.

"The key is in the top drawer of my desk."

"Get it," he says, and puts both hands back on the shotgun, although now he's holding it more like a bouquet than a gun.

I creep up, unfurl myself to full height. I keep my arms out at my side but don't raise them, as if I'm playing defense in basketball. I stand before my desk and whip open the top drawer like I do probably twenty times a day.

"Not so fast," he says, and when I look at him, he glares at me but his hands jump along the barrel like spooked birds.

"Sorry," I say, and rummage through the drawer, among Altoids tins and Luna bars, until I find the makeshift paper clip keychain. Conscious this time of my speed, I glide the drawer shut and hold my open palm out to him, key in the center.

"You do it," he says, and I circle the desk with the caution I'd use around a jittery dog. I pass by him and my back prickles with vulnerability. I turn the key in the lock, calm and controlled. I pull the heavy drawer out and take a step back.

"It's Robertson," he says, and I hope there's more than one Robertson.

I step forward to the file cabinet and flip to the Rs: Rago, Ramirez, Rauch, Reedhovel, Riker, Rivera, Roach, Roberts, Robertson. Only one. For a split second, I consider giving him Roberts, but I don't. I use both hands to pull out the heavy manila folder.

By its weight alone, I would know this analysis is done. New patients only have the questionnaire and letters of consent, ten sheets of paper at most. This file bulges with secrets.

I hold out the file with two hands, and hope like hell that he will have to use both hands to take it.

He grabs it with one hand. His face contorts; he's so close to having his answers that it's almost painful to watch him work it out.

"Sit down," he says, and waves at the rug with the gun. I sink to my knees and keep my toes curled under me so I can take off at any second. I'd run but he crosses the room and stands between the chairs and my desk, me and the door. He's not looking at me any more; he's only looking at the file.

He's still got his right hand entwined around the trigger of the shotgun, but I don't think he could fire. He can't aim, anyway. The nose of the shotgun droops to the floor as he opens the folder. He hasn't shown relief or dismay yet, so I'm guessing there's no copy of the patient letter that explains the test results. The pages from the lab use medical jargon; it'll take him a while to decipher them.

He looks up at me again and I can see the blood spread through his cheeks. "Head down," he says, and waves the gun at me like a club.

I start to obey but I know he's sucked in by the file, the lure of the unknown made real. His eyes drop and the gun drops and I take my chances.

I throw myself forward to charge past him, but there's not enough room between him and the desk. I miss and glance off his shoulder. The barrel of the shotgun presses against the outside of my hip like an unwanted erection as I stumble away. From the open record in his hand, half a sheaf of paper wafts to the floor; there's no way I can grab any of it.

"Hey," he says, as startled as I am by my heroics, but I am past him and I am not stopping now. He yells as I go out the door. I hear clatter as he bangs into something, probably those chairs whose legs are too spindly to be true waiting room chairs, but I run without looking down the covered walkway. I'm glad I wore Mary Jane sneakers instead of flip-flops today.

There's nobody in sight to ask for help. I pound around the corner, across the parking lot to the strip mall and the Jamba Juice I walk to most days on break. Only when I'm slowed by the hydraulic push of the door do I look behind me: he's not there. He's not following me.

I have survived.

I'm thrilled. I feel giddy. My heart's pounding from the run and from the sheer joy that I am alive; I have escaped an ordeal unscathed. I have not been raped. I have not been killed. Hallelujah.

I march to the counter, cutting in front of two blondes in velour tracksuits and an old man in bike shorts. The blondes make catty comments to each other and the old man is mid-order, but I don't even process that as I say to the guy in the paper hat behind the counter, "I just got held up by a guy with a shotgun and I need to call the cops."

There is a moment of silence while the paper hat guy opens and closes his mouth, then says, "Like, mugged?"

"I couldn't grab any of it," I say.

"Are you all right?" the old biker guy says, obviously more together than the paper hat guy, and I nod.

"Yes. Not mugged. Held up. I work at Daybreak Labs around the corner, in the Medford Offices, you know, that way," I say, and wave my arm but I don't care which direction, "and a guy came in with a shotgun and said he'd kill me if I cooperated, I mean, didn't cooperate."

"Terrible," the old biker guy says.

"Whoa," Paper Hat says. His co-worker comes from the back to listen to me.

The blondes squeal behind me, but the old biker guy is calm. "Here, use my cell," he says. "You should lock the doors," Old Biker says to the Jamba Juice guys. "Just in case." Paper Hat produces a key ring, turns the deadbolt in the double doors.

My hands won't work and I misdial twice before Old Biker says, "Let me. It's tricky." I feel grateful for this kindness. The air conditioning is cool on my face and arms.

The conversation with 911 flies by. They tell me to stay put, that officers will come. They ask if some strange number is my cell number, and I say no. They ask where they can reach me and I realize my purse is in my desk.

"Did he take your bag?" Paper Hat asks once I'm off the phone. I know he heard me tell the cops where my phone is.

"No, it's at work," I say. "In my desk."

"It's gone now," Paper Hat says, and I feel less triumphant, suddenly foolish, when one of the blondes comes to my defense.

"Moron, of course she left it," she says, and she looks regal in raspberry velour. "You give them whatever they want so you never go to the second location."

"And you never get in the car," her friend in a less-becoming apricot says.

"That's the second location thing," Raspberry says.

A blender whirs to life and scares the bejeezus out of me. I jump into the side of Old Biker. He puts a hand on my arm and pats me like he's not going to tell anyone my secrets.

"Sorry," Paper Hat's co-worker says. He looks at me and although he didn't see me freak, he sees Old Biker comforting me. "I thought you could use an Immuno Blaster."

"Why don't you sit down," Old Biker says, and I let him guide me to a chair. He sits cattycorner from me.

"I tried to stop him," I say. "But I couldn't. So I ran."

"That's very brave."

"I had to give him the file, you know?"

"The file?"

"He wanted medical records. Someone else's medical records." Old Biker might be mystified, but he's letting me talk. "The lab is in midtown, and they have security there, but not in our office."

"I think that may change," Old Biker says.

"It better," I say, "before I go back. He had a shotgun, and I don't argue with people with shotguns." The others hover around the front door, peering into the street for the wackadoo or the police. Since they're looking, I feel like I don't have to. Heaven sent smoothie-swilling guardian angels to watch over me.

"No, no."

"Just a panic button would be good, to call the cops? My boss put panic buttons in the lab but I don't think anyone's ever tried to steal records before. Nobody knows where our office is." I feel like a wind-up toy that's running down: jabber, jabber, jabber.

"What kind of tests do you do?"

"I can't imagine it's that much to put a panic button in, right? They should be able to do that easy." I look at Old Biker and realize he asked me a question. I think he works with kids, teenagers. His eyes show patience with my babbling.

"Tests? Oh, things people don't want showing up on their insurance," I say.

"Like what?" Old Biker presses, and I have to focus to answer his question.

"Like, if someone wants to find out if they're carrying genes for breast cancer but they don't want their insurance to kick them out or raise their premiums if they are." Or if they don't want anyone to know they've had a test done.

Paper Hat's co-worker hands me a smoothie. "No charge."

"Thanks." I suck it down, frozen mango and orange. Co-Worker gives me a flirty look but I am not in the mood. I ignore him and keep talking to Old Biker until Co-Worker returns to the door. "So we do tests like cancer marker stuff, drug tests, DNA, blood types."

"For criminal analysis?"

"No, my boss doesn't like testifying." In my mind, I see his hands twitching over the barrel of the gun. Would he really have shot me for a file?

"Pregnancy tests?" Old Biker asks. I think about Liz and wonder where she is now. Tuesday mornings she teaches at her daughter's co-op preschool, but she was supposed to have her thirty-five-week ultrasound today to see if the new tater tot was breech.

"No, the pee-on-a-stick tests are good and cheap. That's what I'm supposed to tell people." A pain point forms in my sinuses; I drank my smoothie too fast.

Old Biker looks out the window then looks back at me. He's waiting for the police to arrive before he leaves me. I must look awful.

"Paternity tests?"

I need to call Liz.

"Yeah," I say, "our biggest seller." The smoothie is sharp and sweet. My teeth ache.

"I bet," he says, and looks out the window again. He'll tell me when the cops get here.

"I should call my boss."

"Here," Old Biker says, and slides his phone across the tabletop to me. "I'll be back. Get you anything?" I shake my head no, and he gets in line.

I punch the number in, hands steady now, and hope she'll pick up the call from an unrecognized number. "Liz," I say when she answers, and I can't think of a better way to say it, "Liz, he knows."

Mother of Pearl

Carolyn Selman

An egret, stilt-legged, statue-still
makes a sudden snatch.
A little splash, a pale flash of prey—
the glint on a worn blade.

Time falls away like peel,
I'm in the garden, four years old,
my grandfather holds out a bright
green apple, grips his pocket knife,
its handle, mother of pearl.
"Who's Pearl's father?"
He laughs. Unclasped, the notched
blade reflects sunlight. Deftly
he carves round and around
the apple. I watch it spin, entranced
as the green ribbon lengthens
into a twisted spiral, falls
in one long, fragile piece,
a soft weight netted in my hands.

A sudden gleam
and a memory breaks the surface
then water closes over it again.

Conversations About the Moon

Eric Johnson

You are one with whom thoughts about the moon cannot pass
without mention. And the conversation we had didn't last
any longer than your asking, Did you see the moon last night?

Of all the nights spent hunkered at the dining room table
or plodding through the plot of a novel, that night, I had
glanced out my window and happened to notice it—
not particularly full or luminous. And I recall, as I turned

my attention back to the novel, to my meal, an awareness
that I had seen the moon and I would remember seeing it,
and if you happened to ask me the next time we met,
I could say yes, yes, I saw the moon.

Small Favors

Judy Hamilton

The scar on the back of my head curves from just over my right ear to the crown and snakes its way to the nape of my neck. Sometimes when it rains, like tonight, it prickles. But I don't touch it because the skin around the scar creeps and crawls like a worm in the throes of a lingering death, reminding me that the cold cut of a knife nearly claimed my own life. The same signal that orders my fingers to stay away awakens a memory of an iron hand closing around my head that rainy night seven years ago, and fear, like the worm, its tiny bristles clawing my skin, burrows deep inside me.

The rain ping-pinged against my office window. I rose from my chair, rubbed my face and gazed out at the darkening sky, then at the traffic mess two stories below. A layer of greenery spreads over San Diego's landscape, hiding the desert floor. Through months of moistureless weather, oil that drips from cars bakes into the asphalt. The slightest rain turns streets into grease pits. Three cars braked, but skidded into each other as the light turned red in the slicked-up intersection. Smack, smack, smack. Bumper cars in the city.

The sky rumbled and I looked up to the flight path directly over my building. An orange and blue 737 came into view, descending to Lindbergh Field down the hill. Lights from Coronado were already twinkling across the harbor. I left the office and drove to Barney's Gun Shop.

"Hey, Barney. Got anything new?"

The police had confiscated my gun, so I test-fired a 92 model Beretta. I had been a good customer for over six years.

After the knife attack, I recuperated in the hospital for a week. At home I slept for another week. But I was always a self-starter. I could just get back to work and things would be normal. I'd live with it. People live with this stuff all the time.

The next day I got up at six and dressed. I went down to the garage and started my car and backed out, and drove back in. I went upstairs and lay down on the couch and watched TV.

I could barely lift my arm to change the channel on the remote. I lay there in my suit and high heels until about two in the afternoon, until it was too late to go to work. I ate something and went to bed.

I did that until I ran out of food. I was cutting off chunks of frozen pot pie when I finally decided to get some groceries. I figured I could do one thing a day, so I gave up taking showers and getting dressed to go to work, and went to the store. I bought Peppermint Patties and Doritos and Cherry Garcia ice cream and ready-made mac and cheese in the deli section. I started feeling pretty good as long as I watched TV and didn't think about anything. At night, when I couldn't sleep, I made a cup of tea with a dollop of rum, or maybe just rum, and listened to Charlie Parker's "Gypsy."

Charlie Parker, "Bird," was almost dead when he made that record in L.A. in 1945. The breath it took to blow each note through a number five reed was hard enough on a good day. Heroin and alcohol and probably a combination of a lot of other things had sapped his strength, but not his will. He always hated that recording. I never paid much attention to it before. Now I can hear the pain in every breath. Days later he ended up at Camarillo State Mental Hospital and he recovered. He was twenty-five years old and lasted ten more years.

I almost died when I was twenty-five and I wanted to last longer than ten years, so I thought it couldn't hurt to see a therapist. The doctor was alert and peered at me with bright bird eyes. He asked what I was feeling and I told him.

"My life doesn't seem my own, at least what I remember my life used to be, or who I used to be."

I went back to work, but not the same work. Not complicated stuff, nothing I had to research or argue about. When I even thought about tax research, it was like a six-ton elephant sitting on my chest, holding another quarter-ton of Internal Revenue Codes and other weighty stuff to flip through.

I earned enough money to eat and drink, preferably scotch, although I didn't care if it was Pinch anymore. I couldn't imagine myself buying that sexy lingerie in my dresser drawers. I just wore the same plain white bra and panties. They got pretty worn with all the washing, and the elastic was loose since I threw them in the dryer, which I never used to do. I tried not to think about how I used to do things.

My old work seemed like a jigsaw puzzle and I couldn't fit the pieces together. What I used to do was put all these things—codes, regulations, court cases—in little compartments in my brain and then a case would come in and I would pick one thing out of this drawer and one out of that drawer and put them together. It was creative, like science or art; maybe it had never been put together like that before. And I was always saying, "Aha." But then my brain became a slob. Things were spilling out of the drawers, like a teenager's room. And things were hiding in there, in my brain—the growling laugh, the nightmares.

Sometimes I would wake up in the night and lie very still, holding my breath, to see if anyone was moving in my room. I wondered if their eyes had adjusted to the light and they could see my eyes open and looking for them. There was never anyone there. But you can't say never, because some night someone might be there. You can't plan on anything being the same as it was before because the next minute hasn't happened yet. The next minute can bring anything.

I tried to stick to a routine. I didn't drive to strange parts of town. If I stayed in Point Loma, it was pretty safe. I didn't have to keep a watch out for bad things happening. Nothing bad much happens in Point Loma. I heard sirens sometimes at night or early in the morning. It seemed they were always going to the submarine base—sailors and trouble went together.

But if I was in a strange place and there was a loud noise, I had to stop what I was doing. My blood vessels jammed up, my heart pounded and I got cold all over, goose bumps. I stood perfectly still, so no one would notice me—not exactly the best camouflage, but I thought looking calm and normal made you blend in. Inside, though, that moment of terror, when what has been done to you in the past can never equal the fear of what might be done to you in the future, comes back full force. My therapist says it's "fight or flight" syndrome, but there are some things you can't fight. You're helpless. You have to suck it up or you won't survive. Each moment like that put me back in that truck, in the rain, in terror.

I miss the feel of someone's arms around me. Over the years I tried losing myself in hot, sweaty, mind-numbing sex, but any night can turn a caress and the touch of a hand into a nightmare of cold hard steel, so I stopped thinking about love or "like."

My therapist opined that I hadn't experienced real tragedy, that someday it would be a sad, but normal memory that wouldn't keep me up at night. But why should I remember? I didn't ask for torture to be part of my life. So I'm working it out on my own. My prescription for therapy is just to forget, go along smoothly. Eventually . . . well, I lost some time, that's all.

The therapist said I should get a hobby, a diversion, something to take my mind off myself.

"I like to cook," I said, thinking of poached pears with creme anglais. "But I live alone. I'd get fat."

"Do you sew? My wife knits up a storm." He opened his suit coat to reveal a gray wool vest with a maroon dog on the front.

"I made a stuffed dog in home ec. Two dogs, actually, gray poodles with tufts of black yarn on their heads and tails. One was a puppy." Warm and fuzzy. I could take those dogs off the top shelf of my closet and just get in bed and snuggle. That would defeat the purpose, I guessed. "I could stop by the yardage shop on the way home and get a pattern. My grandmother's sewing machine is in the garage."

I drove past the yardage shop on my way out of downtown. I took the frontage road alongside the freeway, so I could stop at El Indio for rolled tacos and guacamole. Without thinking I pulled into the parking lot of a square tan building. The salesman was waiting on a beefy man in a leather jacket, so I looked at the display in the glass counter. *Pretty*, I thought. Black, silver, pearl inlays. Some were displayed on the wall behind the counter. I smelled cigarette breath behind me.

"Lookin' for something?" The salesman's voice was gravelly.

I pointed.

"Good eye."

"Can I try it out?"

He opened a drawer for the accessories and led me through a heavy metal door. The room was long and narrow, the air thick and metallic. He handed me two orange foam nuggets which I stuck in my ears. My blood hammered in the utter silence.

Blam. Bull's eye.

"Shit, ma'am. Try that again."

Blam. Blam. Blam.

"You're a natural, babe."

I felt my mouth curve up in an out-of practice smile. Warm and fuzzy.

The salesman pulled out a sleek black case for the 9mm Glock and explained about the red laser eye. I signed up for lessons as he filled a sack with enough ammo to start a small war.

That night I lay in bed with the Glock under my pillow. Glorious, dreamless sleep washed over me. I woke to the sound of birds chirping in the jacaranda tree outside my window. I laced up my Nikes and fast-walked a mile to fisherman's landing on the bay. I breathed in fog and sea air, and listened to seagulls *auk auk* above my head. I bought a cup of coffee, black, from the old salt running the dockside café, and sat on a stool watching fishing boats jostle side to side, up and down on the incoming tide. In no time he was calling me "Miss Dee," and my butt was in fine shape.

I referred all my clients to other attorneys in exchange for them sending me some nice, normal people who needed wills or trusts, not that nice, normal people don't get in trouble with the IRS. But from now on there would be no conflict for me. I would meet with clients who led normal lives, with loving families and enough money to need an estate plan. They would be happy people who didn't cower in fear every time the phone rang. They paid their bills on time and actually looked forward to opening their mail. They talked about their above-average sons and daughters on their way to Princeton or UC Santa Barbara.

During the day I met with pleasant ladies and gentlemanly men, busied myself with A and B trusts and charitable giving. I turned away anyone with a problem—greedy children, greedy ex-wives. There's a lot of greed in the estate planning business, but there are plenty of happy, thoughtful families who just want to get their lives in order so they won't be a burden on their loved ones when their time comes.

And after work I stopped by Barney's Gun Shop. The owner thought it strange that I practiced in a suit and high heels, but I figured that's how I was going to be dressed if I ever needed to fire my weapon.

Blam. Blam. Blam. I moved up from circle targets to people outlines. Some days I drew cocky fedoras and bushy mustaches on the outline with a Magic Marker before sending it back down the shooting lane. Sometimes I drew a fancy-buckled belt and lowered my aim.

On The Edge

Roger Aplon

The maple leaves have begun to turn. There's been no rain.

On Valencia Street the toothless beggar snoozes in the shade of the painter's awning.

Boys & girls from the parochial school around the corner flirt & kiss in the park across the way. *It's 3 o'clock*

She'd announced the end last week & he's been drunk ever since. Begins juicing before even the alarm.

The car she drives is fast, comfortable, filled with ghosts & goes only where she directs.

The fables that sprung-up around the table tell of lovers crossed & the terror of a gun in the wrong hands. *It's Midnight*

No one seems to notice the singer in the flowered slip who's slit her wrists & dances slowly marking her way.

In New York City at *4 AM* the lady of the house cannot sleep. She wanders & sips her potion,

the one with vodka, mint & sassafras . . . the one with the black seed at the center.

5 AM & all is quiet on front street except for the staccato slap/slap/ slap (thigh against thigh) as the neighbor's daughter entertains her man.

& if we look for him, the boozer, he's asleep on his fire escape. In his dream, he has little left . . .

Sunrise soon

74,500 People Die in an Earthquake
on October 8, 2005 in Pakistan. There are Children Buried Under the Weight of Collapsed Schools

Pattie Wells

"Village schools collapse, burying
children in earthquake rubble." Ash and snow

shroud, delicate flakes
float into a stanza, black spots

on a patchwork snow.
Mothers in hijabs dig through debris, cut

tamarisk trees, cook water
and Biriani rice. (I am just trying—

in a daydream—to step gently
over dead bodies.)

The injured and the old. How curious,
they smile when they see an American.

They share photos of their missing
children. If aid does not arrive soon,

they will become winter's buried angels.
They are like us, their muse

speaks to them about pain,
in words now written in the snow.

Now the word disappears.

Baby, It's You

Judy Geraci

Stepping off the Metroline onto Wilshire Boulevard, I try to imagine myself as I hope others see me: lanky, loose-limbed, like a basketball player strolling off the court to play it cool in front of the lay-deez. Being tall in Westwood has a great advantage among the throngs of office workers, shoppers, students, and the general mass of humanity swarming the sidewalks. Being half-Indian helps me blend in, not because I'm wily and good at tracking, but because here I'm another multicultural longhair, with my backpack and headphones.

For an environmentally sensitive young man like me, the Westwood-Wilshire cross is brutal: exhaust fumes, brake dust, and ear-punishing sirens. Who could blame me for wanting to kick some manicured metro-man booty? But at my height, just over 6'3, I am able to take a benevolent view. Moving along to the beat of my own soundtrack, The Rolling Thunders, I feel especially expansive today. No reason in partic—just feeling the love all around me.

I see the high-heeled, linen-suited woman, satchel on shoulder, and the big crimson stain across the back of her pin-tucked skirt. I feel for her. I walk past a trio of well-dressed Middle Eastern men hawking gold jewelry and feel the worry behind their boastful cries. I especially feel for the bearded Muslim who I pass almost every day at lunch, with his sandwich sign propped on the sidewalk before him. Early in the week it says HUNGRY, then advances to VERY HUNGRY, or STARVING.

Usually I shake my head, on to this con artist. But today, I see him for who he really is. A stately priest with Arabic features, African skin and white wool flocking down from his multi-mirrored prayer cap, past his closed eyes, bordering each side of his hollow jaw, and on from his chin to his breastbone. I drop a five in the bowl at his feet, where a new sign announces: FAMISHED. The man, without opening his eyes, says, "Thank you." Surprised to hear him speak, I stutter, "You're welcome." He gives a tip of the head, which I decide to receive as a blessing upon me. Just how did I hear that thank you through my headphones, I wonder, as I peer back over my shoulder to take one last look. The man has disappeared.

For a sec, I feel super weird—lightheaded, a bit out-of-body and wondering about what the hell is up. But I know it's all co-inky-dink; he probably went to get food. I'm feeling a little high on life, is all, or maybe it's something I inhaled off the bus, but I am not delusional. I adjust my headphones, dial Echo and the Bunnymen into the perfect volume, and regain my stride. Which lasts about two minutes, until I feel a tug, then a stronger pull at my shirt sleeve. My music's blasting, and I stare at a face mouthing my name in rhythm. It's a familiar face with familiar fuzzy eyebrows rising in ecstatic parentheses. I pull out my headphones and listen.

"Roanhorse, is that really you?" the familiar voice gushes.

It's kinda hard to focus with all these people swooshing together and drifting apart like clouds around me. But that face, how could I have hesitated for even a split second? If you ever need to define the word beatific, just point to Sherry. At forty-something, she's got this long, silver-blond hair, wide grin, huge flared nostrillicus, flushed face like she just finished a great big O, and that voice fluttering up and down like a raisin in the champagne bubbles. But mainly it's her eyes—wide-set, open in a state of perpetual pleasure and surprise. Like she's awake but still streaming through a flying dream, or maybe just still cold-trippin' from her best acid trip ever.

"Oh. Wow! Sherry!" With my rhythm broken, I have to rummage around my head for normal conversation. All I manage is another, "Wow! Sherry!" until finally my brain farts out, "What an amazing coincidence. How are you? What are you doing here?"

Back in Tri-City, we were friends. Well, as much as you could be friends with a psychotic patient when you weren't one yourself. I'd worked part-time as an aide for the last year before I came back to school. She was always the best dressed, with a new matching outfit every day. But last time I saw her she was mewling on all fours in the laundry closet, scratching and snarling at anyone who tried to lure her away from the nest she'd made of sheets and towels to birth her litter. I left about four days after that, but heard through some former co-workers that her parents discharged the conservator they'd hired. Mom and Dad pulled some strings and greened some palms to get her transferred back to the expensive, hush-hush, Beverly Hills sanatorium where she'd started out. How she ever ended up in the pit of Tri-City is still a mystery to me.

"You know I live here now, well actually in Brentwood," she says. "Of course, not right here in the middle of the sidewalk, although, you know people do, and it could just as easily be me. But right now, by the grace of, well you-know-who, I'm doing great, feeling really good."

We step aside to let a tour group of high schoolers wearing "Born to be Bruin" T-shirts pass us. My sight snags on the overweight teacher scuffling behind them—a toilet paper flag waving out the back of his khaki's. I flash a merciful vibe his way.

"Yeah, well you look great, Sherry. Really good."

And she did look better than ever with her designer sweat suit and her hair pulled back into a clasp of semi-precious something. She fit right in the Westwood mix, like she'd just stepped out of The Beautiful Nail. Except if you really looked, something was a little off; her eyes a little too spaced-out, her smile stretched out a little too Muppety. Still, she had this glow that you couldn't ignore.

This may show how hard up I was in those Tri-City days, or how cool she could be when her meds were working. When my shift was slow, we talked. She kept telling me that I was too good for the place, that I was smart enough to get a PhD if I wanted. She crushed on me, I guess. I don't think I really encouraged it. I was just trying to treat her, you know, like a human being. Once she asked if I would ever date her, if we were on the outside. I thought she meant in theory—like, was she someone who was ask-outable? So, of course, I wanted her to know there was somebody out there who would want her. I mean, she was way too old for me anyhow. Or at least that's what I kept telling myself. Because even with her age and her disability and all, I still felt this strange kind of pull. If you asked me straight out, I'd deny it totally. But at times I'd find myself staring, wondering what she was like before she wigged out, how she'd looked before the baby. Truthfully, if it weren't for her huge belly, I might've been fighting unprofessional urges.

But she always brought it up. "After I have the baby, I'm going to really work out and get my shape back. And then I'll be able to take my old meds, and you won't even recognize me. When I get out, maybe we could get together, go have coffee, catch a movie or something." But as I knew, as her chart and everyone else knew, Sherry had been "pregnant" for at least two years. Somehow she convinced herself and her body cooperated, maintaining the bloat of a six-month pregnancy.

The pregnancy—I'd forgotten. I try to counter the pull of my eyes from her stomach, but they are fixed tight on the amazingly flat plain of her abdomen. Unable to will my eyes, I jerk my whole head up, but too late, she's already seen me.

"They tried to tell me it was a pseudocyesis." She smiles and rubs her belly in circles.

"A suit-a-what? I'm sorry, I'm a little lost here," I say, looking for a place to set my eyes.

She laughs bells. "Oh, Roanhorse, you are still so funny. Pseudocyesis—spurious pregnancy, hysterical pregnancy, false pregnancy. To explain it as they did to me about a thousand times, it's the condition in which a female believes herself to be pregnant and develops all clinical pregnancy signs in the absence of a real pregnancy. Almost every symptom of a true pregnancy except no heart tones or visible fetus. Key word—visible—you know? Or was it viable? Anyhow, the doctors can't tell without an ultrasound. Even the hormone levels change to pregnant ones."

I shut my mouth and try to think an answer, searching for clues in the crowd. Heading toward us, a pair of balding professors argue in sign language, their hands scribbling fast on invisible whiteboards.

"Wow, that's bizarre," I finally say. "So how *did* they explain it?"

She beams a smile that tugs up the corners of my own mouth. "Oh, you know, they have all their theories, and of course one psychiatrist contradicts another. Let's see—there's conflict theory where the fear of pregnancy creates an internal conflict and causes the endocrine systems to go bonkers. Then there's wish-fulfillment theory where you want to be pregnant, so you get the symptoms, then you think you're pregnant and get more symptoms. And then there's always major depressive disorder to explain anything they can't explain. Have I ever looked depressed to you?"

She cracks another of those incredible contagious smiles and I feel its mirror image transpose itself onto my own lips. But the smile turns serious as she lowers her voice. "Except they finally admitted that in some cases they do find a petrified blastocyst, a fetal demise that leaves only its fossil. Isn't that freaky? But mine . . . mine was still breathing."

"Wow. Freaky." I nod though I haven't followed a single word she's said. "So are you saying that you were actually, uh, expecting?"

She grins and nods her head yes.

"So then, how . . . what?"

Sherry waits for a gaggle of super-tan sorority sisters to pass, then whispers, "Have you heard of psychic surgery? It's the latest thing—virtually a miracle." She grabs my arm, hooks her elbow in mine, and begins walking me toward campus.

Visions of Geraldo, masked and gowned, pulling a bloody chicken liver from some fatty's intact stomach swim in front of me. Psychic surgery, gawd. How old was that? Sherry baby, stuck in time same as ever. I imagine the extravagant set up, the involved staging to relieve her of the pseudo-baby—all the bloat and gas of psychoses.

"Are you telling me they did some kind of supernatural, uh, intervention?"

"With your heritage, Roanhorse, I knew you'd understand. It's fortunate that you left when you did, though, with all the stories spreading about us."

"Stories?"

"You know, some people think I'm promiscuous just because I came into my womanhood without all those sexual stereotypes and uptight hang-ups. But you'd never say I'm promiscuous, right?"

Her voice is rising, and catches the ears of a passing group in hospital gear. One guy in greens holds up his stethoscope in mock attention, while the woman next to him laughs too loudly.

I forgive her sexual insecurity, hiding behind her teddy bear smock. I try to imagine myself in her place. Which is easier than imagining the next passers-by—dudes my age—power-walking suits packing *Wall Street Journals* under their arms. I pull in close. "Sherry, I promise, I would never say you were promiscuous."

"Roanhorse, sometimes I think you're an Earth Angel. You are, aren't you?"

Oh no, here we go again, I'm thinking. Wooo whooo. Wacky-talk time.

"You mean like the song?" I burst out into a little falsetto. "'Earth Angel.'"

"Did you know that's the number one first-dance song at weddings?" I am babbling, hoping to switch tracks, get her out of that territory.

"There are angels here on earth, you know, to help us with our problems." Her crystal blue eyes lock on mine. "It's true."

"Yeah?" I'm breathing in and out my nose, lips pressed so I don't laugh. I wonder if she sees me with a big feather headdress or shaman white paint.

"Do you believe that, Roanhorse?"

"Oh gosh, Sherry, I don't know. I had a friend once who gave me this book about *Meet Your Angels* and all that. Tried to teach me an exercise to find my wings and all—but to tell you the truth, I never could get into it."

Light goes out of her eyes.

"But that doesn't mean anything, I mean, I'm a cynic, you know, all around." Light flickers on.

"Yeah, what matters is if it works for you. No different than Jesus Christ or Holy Moses, Vishnu or Great Spirit."

"Yes, exactly!" She speeds up, fully animated. "An Earth Angel came to me in the body of Dr. Zelwick Vorkowski. He had knowledge, an old Romanian technique they used to help the unborn Jewish babies escape the Holocaust so they could be born later on in safety. My parents had connections and . . . I know it's unbelievable to most people, but I had a spiritual abortion, and the baby got to move on to a good place, a real good place."

I'm feeling a little disoriented, suddenly, as I see the ancient one pass by again. He's holding what appears to be a white dove in his hand.

"Are you okay? You look a little shaken. I know it's a pretty intense thing to hear about our baby."

Okay, I admit, I'm tripping wildly at this point, but all this Earth Angel business on a day like today, has really knocked me off balance. I do a double take and see that the dove is actually a falafel wrapped in white paper. Deep breath, I tell myself. I reach for my ponytail and run my fingers through the smooth black to the rough split ends, just to feel grounded. Then I'm back, rock steady.

"*Our* baby? Uh, Sherry, you know we never, I never . . . ." Suddenly, I'm starting to question myself—I mean, I know about counter-transference and all that, but just because you have a fantasy or two doesn't mean you actually did it and forgot.

She pats my shoulder. "That's okay, I understand. Hey, you never did tell me what you're studying. I assume you're getting your doctorate in psychology, right? Isn't that what you were after? Tri-City was just a stopping place to get your feet wet, I suppose Well, I hope they gave you a good scholarship."

She's suddenly cogent again. Who knows why. Just the way it works.

"Um, actually, I decided to go to nursing school instead. I'm still working part-time as an aide though—UCLA pays pretty well, at least compared to Tri-City. That's where I was going just now. I'm on in an hour. In fact, I probably need to stop and get something to eat." I hold my hand up to my brow to survey the scene. "Indian Palace, Indian Princess, Pride of India—all these Indian restaurants and no fry bread to be found!"

She ignores my joke. "You're kidding? UCLA psych ward? How come I've never seen you? That's where my one of my best friends is staying. You must have heard of him, Gary Dennis?"

I shake my head. "No, actually, they put me in the Neonatal ICU. I help out with the preemies."

"Oh, of course, of course. It makes perfect sense after all that's happened. But still, you may have heard of Gary—he impersonated a gynecologist. I told him it wasn't a good idea, but he didn't mean anything. He's a socially backward, though, too shy to get girls the usual way."

I have to work hard to not roll my eyes. I'm starting to get worn out by Sherry and I need to save some spirit for the babies.

"Well, Sherry," I make solid eye contact and smile. "It's been real good talking to you. It's great to see you doing so well." My foot turns the forty-five degree angle that says it's time.

"Oh, Roanhorse," she says, "it's been an absolute pleasure. I'm sure we'll certainly run into each other again. My folks live just around the bend. Well, *au revoir*."

I nod and give her the peace sign, thinking about all the different routes I'll have to take in the future, which bus stops, the back roads. Still, though . . . whose song now crawls around my hairless ears? I swear something always happens when Sherry starts up the old *Angels in the Outfield* theme. Every song blends together in my head like some wild 1950s' mix—"Sherry Baby," "Baby it's You," the Sherilles, and now it's the Penguins. And as much as I scorn all that crystal-gazing, vortex-aligning, spirit-guiding crappola, and the way all the new-agers have taken over Sedona, and Hallmark's selling Kokopelli, I still wonder. Why, after all this time, did Sherry have to pop out front today?

Yeah, I've seen the movies—*Wings of Desire, Heaven Can Wait*—and I get totally into them and all. But so do a ton of people and that doesn't mean we all actually believe in the stuff. I mean, who's gonna buy an earthbound angel as the predestined soul mate of a psychotic person? So why, Sherry Baby, is there warm syrup spilling maple through my chest? Why did you cause that tingle under my shoulder blades, like feathers unzipping? Why the upbreeze, that lift I've been feeling all day?

"Those first days . . . she always found herself alone when the weather broke."

— Michael Ondaatji, *Anil's Ghost*

Breaking the Weather

Lizzie Wann

it is not quite summer
    and she is distracted
    her clothes tumble
    for 10 minutes
    for only 25 cents
    and she remembers
    watching him untie his new lover's scarf
    the relief of her neck
    where he would bury his face later
    and the weather changes
    in such small moments

she reaches her right hand
    over her left shoulder
    presses her fingers into the muscles
    of her back
    this is where her storms begin & end

she has memorized the location
    massages it when she feels the clouds gathering
    it is the place where she directs her chaos
    as if you can control the hurricane
    as if the knowledge of its arrival
    will somehow make you safer

Rain

Margot Wilding

What relief, to be neither chosen nor expendable. Everything is drenched. Water finds the low places—here I want to say *chooses*, as if rain decides. Mind's sky holds the old horizons, earth's buckles and heaves, the exponents of green. Torrents pour from porch eaves, the porch no longer there, the whole plot bare but for locust trees and mulberries—and this languorous melancholy, exotic and fickle as funny weather— like playing dolls with sadness—

holding her by the waist, walking her across the worn boards, placing words in her dour mouth—little silver hosts. Then the gift of transubstantiation—a shift of mood.

Rain itself is mystery: when will it come again, and where, and this loneliness, lustrous, close to erotic, like watching thoughts of you drift upmind—no *next time* promise, no wave, no why.

Cecil

Sandra Joss

Cecil is eager to share his story with me. In an unabashed way, this sixty-year-old man tells of childhood struggles that have become his metaphor for life. His trust in me, and his story, captures my heart. And yet, revealing his wounds in such a candid way seems to contradict his indirect demeanor. As he talks, he never looks at my face, his forehead down, looking at the ground. A photo-op changes that, but only briefly. Now, as I look at his image—gray, frizzy hair rising as static electricity from his head, and the unsmiling face—I feel a twinge of guilt: Cecil is one of the "Stolen Children."

Until recently, most white Australians were unaware of the prolonged episode in Australian history in which thousands of indigenous children were forcibly removed from their families by government authorities. For the most part, children were removed for no other reason than their Aboriginality. This practice began in the late nineteenth century. In some states it did not stop until the late seventies.

The children who were taken away are known as the "Stolen Children" or the "Stolen Generations." Many Aboriginal people continue to be deeply affected by this practice, central to which was the attempted severance of language and culture. For many artists with whom I worked the "Stolen Generations" experience is real. They have had grandparents, parents, extended family, or themselves taken from their family homes and institutionalized.

This is Cecil's story:

I'm about the oldest bloke here (Eora Arts Centre in Sydney) . . . these young fellas ask a lot of questions about the history. I don't know too much about the history 'cause I was locked away. And even after I got out of the Homes I got into a lot of trouble. I'd say I spent over thirty years in jail. That's where I done a lot of painting. I was in Long Bay Jail, Goulburn, Bathurst, Cessnock, Maitland, Parramatta. . . . I wasn't painting all the time, just the later years. I'm pretty lucky in a way, 'cause

I am an alcoholic, but I'm a sober alcoholic and it took me a few years to give that away.

I was born in Cowra about 200 miles west of Sydney. I was taken away as a baby by the Australian Government and put into a home down the South Coast near Nowra—Bomaderry Children's Home. I was there till I was ten. Then I was taken up to Kinchela Home at Kempsey and I was there till I was eighteen. I came down to Sydney then, and more or less call Redfern home.

I remember my father, when I was the age of walking, coming to Bomaderry Children's Home to get us out. Still in his soldier's uniform, he'd just got back from the War [WW II]. There was me, my sister a bit older, and a younger brother. But they wouldn't let us go. I felt rotten about him until I got to Redfern.

I started running into people who said they were related to me. And one bloke said, "You ought to go to Cowra and see your old man." I didn't believe it. I'd always thought I was an orphan. You know it was a pretty big shock to me. I did go to Cowra. We didn't have too much in common, you know. I never grew up with him around. He was Aboriginal. See, apparently my mother died with my younger brother when he was born and that's when I was taken. I was about eighteen months old.

The whole time I was in the Home they said I had no parents.

A story told this spontaneously and simply, so apparently straight from the heart, must be authentic. Does the telling of his story ease Cecil's pain? Or does it only reinforce his anger over the government's past treatment of Aboriginal people?

Cecil's story is discomfiting. Maybe that's the way it should be.

It's about eleven o'clock in the morning, a sunny, warm Thursday, when my sister, Lyn, and I arrive at Redfern train station. The Aussie locals keep saying we're having an Indian summer, that mid-March is unseasonably warm. I've just left winter in the United States so I'm not set to complain. This day, we are heading to Waterloo (like Redfern, an inner-city suburb of Sydney) to check out two new indigenous art galleries.

As we leave the station, I notice a group of men standing on the other side of the road, in front of a building called CentreLink.

They are a motley crew indeed, all shapes and sizes. But one of the men seems familiar. Turning to Lyn, I say, "See that group of men over there? One of them looks like Cecil, one of the art students I interviewed, and spent time with. But I'm not sure." The bushy grey-black hair standing up and out from his head as if charged with static is what I remember about him. But his physique seems trim and fit, more youthful than I remember.

Lyn points out that pensioners pick up their pension checks from CentreLink. Perhaps that is what these men are doing. She senses my anxiety. So we cross the road. Just then, the men leave their corner and cross the side road, heading towards a special bus, which they proceed to get on. I start to panic. I can't lose Cecil now, if this is he. I call out, "Cecil," and he turns toward me. I smile and wave. It is Cecil after all. He starts to cross the road toward me and just misses getting hit by an oncoming car. (Oh Lord, I don't need that!)

I introduce myself. Perhaps he might remember me from when I interviewed him at Eora Arts Centre several years ago. He seems vaguely aware of that interview, and my presence at Eora. But I see no sign of absolute recall on his face. I start to talk about the book I'm working on, and as I begin he turns away to look at the bus. Everyone is now on board. I see worry in his eyes; he does not want to miss the bus. In a calm voice (remarkably so in retrospect) I say, "You want to catch the bus, don't you."

"Yes, I've got to go. But get in touch with me through Eora," he replies. And off he is, onto the bus. Then he is gone.

To understand my anxiety at seeing Cecil go, before I can hand him a permission slip, before I can get his agreement to use his words and art in my book, you must first know just how difficult it is to locate some of the artists with whom I worked. Indigenous artists are a transient lot; even if they are reasonably successful in marketing or exhibiting their work, they don't seem to stay in the one place for long. To my surprise, I find that getting a current mobile phone number is a good way to get hold of them. But this doesn't work for Cecil. Not only does he not have a phone (mobile or home), but no one knows of his address. And I know that Eora Arts Centre cannot help me for, in truth, Cecil doesn't go there anymore.

I feel a mix of euphoria and disappointment. I have found Cecil. What a joy, and he looks remarkably well, too. And then he is gone; gone before I can share with him that his story as a child of the "Stolen Generations," which I have incorporated into my book, really is important for the wider community to hear; and gone before I have gotten his agreement to use his story and his art.

Just before I leave Sydney to return to the United States an artist tells me about an Aboriginal pastor in Redfern who might be able to help locate Cecil. When I call him, he agrees to give the permission request form to Cecil, when and if he sees him. Of course, it's up to Cecil if he signs the form and puts it in the stamped, addressed envelope to me in San Diego.

The envelope looks as if it has gone through a wringer: it's dirty, torn at one end, and the stamp's half falling off. It's the only mail in the mailbox, which seems sort of strange, not even an advertisement to keep it company. The postmark is Sydney, Australia, and I immediately recognize my printing on the envelope. I rip it open—no time for a neat tear—and unfold the permission form inside, my heartbeat increasing with each second. And then I smile. Cecil agrees to share his story and his art.

History

Crystal Hadidian

From the north side of the street
it was clear: man in bowler hat
at fault, or the poppies;
they certainly beckoned his attention
with arched petals, glossed lips.

But from the apartment across the street—
east corner balcony, a row of neglected potted plants
under a blue and white striped awning
like a crumpled beach towel tossed
over the corner of the building
—from there: it was the woman's fault.
The poppies had nothing to do with it.

San Diego at 1 a.m.

Meagan Marshall

I drove south on the 5—
sliding insensately by like water,
through the 8 east—
to the 15 with glass cracked
One. Big. Glum. Circle,
dead of night drying salt
rivets on my jelled neck.

Billboard promises present and pass
like new—like another city I happened
to be just sailing through,
the side show its usual yet
shifted, this time I sunk in
the la-di-da houses,
one long insuck of thin breath—
mustard Shells, row of palms, plexi-green dot,
as I shot through the cool black
    trying to get back into your light.

Beginning at the End

(From *Boom Dreams*)

Stephen W. Potts

I don't tell Dr. Renssalaer that his flowers are whispering.

I am seated in the padded chair in front of his antique reproduction wooden desk, my legs crossed, my hands folded in my lap. He is saying, "I really believe that you're ready to rejoin the world outside."

I cannot understand what the flowers are saying.

"Of course, I'd be lying to you if I told you that everything will be easy," says Renssalaer. "I wouldn't recommend trying to push yourself too hard—until you've finished your adjustment period. I wouldn't normally be so blunt, but you're an intelligent guy, and I think you have a good grasp of the realities."

I nod acknowledgement of his remark before glancing again at the corner of his desk to my right. The cluster of four flowers stands in a slender glass vase there; they are yellow, something from the narcissus family. I catch one just ceasing to speak with its petal trumpet and lowering the slender leaf it has used to direct its whisper. I nudge my head back toward Renssalaer, directing my stare to the soft green blotter on his desk while keeping the flowers in the corner of my eye.

"And, of course," he continues, "we'll be touching base every couple of weeks until you're off medication."

Glimpsing animate movement, I glance sideways again. One flower leans at an unlikely angle, though now still.

"Is something wrong, Michael?"

My eyes snap to Renssalaer. "Why do you ask?" I say, on guard.

"You were frowning."

"I, uh—I'm sorry," I say. "I was just trying to remember what these flowers are called."

"Of course: that's Jeff and Janet," I imagine him replying. "The one furthest from you is Rafael, and . . ."

But what he really says is, "They're pretty, aren't they? I think they're daffodils. They grow wild around here this time of year."

That explains what they are doing on the desk.

Discreetly, I fix my eyes on Renssalaer's as he finishes his farewell speech. He wears an open-necked dress shirt with broad pastel stripes. He is about my age—around forty-five—and bald on top, while I am silver-sided. But he seems older than me, perhaps because he has authority, perhaps because parts of me are still locked in time loops cycling back into the past. His rimless glasses—my own have wire rims—flash a reflection of the window-framed spring sunlight. The windows in this office are screenless.

"Remember all we've discussed in the last month," says Renssalaer. "Try not to take things so seriously. Keep telling yourself it's going to be all right."

I nod. *Don't you know it's gonna be—all right,* sang John Lennon in "Revolution" twelve years before he was shot. It probably *is* all right in the reality where he survived. But I am trapped in *this* reality.

"So, tell me again," he resumes. "What are you going to be doing at your parents' house?"

"Some reading and writing," I answer. "Get my old job back, if I can. If not, look for another job in a library or bookstore."

"Good, good," says Renssalaer, folding his hands on his desk and slowly nodding.

"After all, if I can't earn enough to move away from my parents, I'll go crazy."

He stares at me, uncertain how to react, until I smile. Realizing it was a joke, he chuckles and drops back in his chair.

"I think you'll do fine," he says. He looks down at the blotter, clearly wondering what to say next. "By the way, do you have one of my personal cards?"

"I don't think so."

As he opens a desk drawer, a large butterfly flaps out of it. It is the size of a hand, papery and brightly painted like a kite. While Renssalaer rummages in the drawer, the butterfly flutters up to the corner of the office over his head.

"Here." He proffers me a white business card. I rise slightly from the seat to take it. I study it a second before thanking him and tucking it in my shirt pocket, taking the opportunity to peek up at the corner. The butterfly has become a rainbow-edged smudge of sunlight just below the angular intersection of walls and ceiling. I trace the reflection to a framed photo on the desktop that has caught a sunbeam falling through the window. I look up again to see the rainbow melt like fading hope.

The rainbow might have had objective existence, but I can find no scientific explanation for the butterfly. Like the whispers of the flowers, it was mine, all mind.

When the call from the receptionist comes informing us that my parents have arrived, Dr. Renssalaer jumps on it. He accompanies me out of the musty aftershave smell of his office into the faintly medicinal one of the corridor. My parents are waiting for me in the reception room, which is furnished in soothing southwestern earth tones: beige, peach, gray, clay, blue. Renssalaer clasps hands with my father. Dad wears a tan sport coat over a pale yellow knit sport shirt. He looks ruddy and healthy, his freckled scalp shining through streamers of brushed back hair.

"How are you?" he says to me, squeezing my shoulder.

"Okay," I answer.

Looking vaguely sad and uncomfortable, my mother steps forward and kisses my cheek.

"Michael," she says.

She wears a green pants suit and plastic-framed glasses. Her hair has about the same proportion of black and white as mine. One side of her mouth still hangs slack from the palsy that hit her a couple of years ago. She had thought it was a stroke. Her face looks older than I remember it, like wrinkled dough, although barely two weeks have passed since I last saw her. But such quantum intervals, with their discontinuities of perception, tend to freeze-frame moments of space-time, bringing change into sharper focus.

As I stare into her face, I see superimposed over it an image of her from one of the photographs that hangs on my parents' bedroom wall: a picture taken in the forties when she was in her early twenties and pretty. As in a movie from that time, her current image suddenly appears black and white with a soft focus. Like film stuck in a projector, it begins to bubble and melt from the center out. I almost look away, afraid of seeing her face grotesquely burned, as it had been during the nuclear war, as it still is in the Grundwelt. But the face I see when the film vaporizes is simply hers in the here and now, corroded with age. It occurs to me that burning and aging are analogous processes of oxidation, part of the price paid for living in earth's oxygen-rich atmosphere. So what I saw is true even if it didn't happen.

Standing in the scoured, earth-toned waiting room, I watch my father engage in small talk with Dr. Renssalaer, joking with him, chuckling and squeezing his elbow to show he is joking. The jokes aren't particularly memorable, but it is Dad's method for putting people at ease; at the moment, he is probably trying to put himself at ease. Renssalaer pretends to be amused; he is accustomed to humoring his patients' family members. I am embarrassed for both of them.

Eager to be out of there, I find myself constructing a time bubble around the scene. I drift back from it, let it slide toward the wrong end of the telescope: Renssalaer, Dad, Mom, warped inside a transparent globe, still moving and talking, though without sound. Like all time bubbles, the globe is not a perfect sphere, but funnels away like melted glass down the corridor of the continuum, out of the institute and onto the highway. I find myself blue-shifting the light at the end of the funnel, preparing to speed my consciousness forward. One decision will take me past the event horizon and set me down several minutes ahead. I worry that it is too soon to abandon the pretenses of the consensuum, before I have even walked out of the institution. I fear that this may not bode well. Perhaps I should have taken all my meds this morning after all.

I think away the time distortion, just in time, as Renssalaer speaks to me.

"You will remember to phone me if you . . . need anything?"

"Of course," I reply.

Dr. Renssalaer shakes my hand. "See you in two weeks then."

On the brink of repeating his words, I stop myself and simply force a smile. Renssalaer shakes my dad's hand. The doctor tells my mother it was nice seeing her again.

The social minuet over, we depart.

In the corridor I hold my breath, holding off the low-probability reality in which Dr. Renssalaer calls me back, apologizing to my parents while announcing that I have been released by mistake.

Outside it is my favorite sort of March day, breezy and faintly moist after the previous week's rains, with mammoth fractal displays of white and gray cumulus crowding each other in the otherwise blue sky. The hills surrounding Bayliss are a bright, organic green—a rare, fleeting hue in Southern California's arid landscape. In fact, the rain has been apocalyptic this winter of 1994-95, leading to quasi-biblical floods and mudslides here in San Diego County. I could not help seeing the weather as an omen that we had collectively collapsed the wrong space-time probability, chosen the wrong branch of reality. We are headed on schedule for the Dark Millenium.

Like so many, my parents shared in that choice themselves, giving their consent to the Newt army and the end of hope. I had warned them; I had tried to warn everyone. Of course, I must have been crazy. I should have known that the truth would trap me.

The parasites from the Enemy still suck invisibly on our reptile brains, controlling the consensuum. I, perhaps alone now, have seen them. I'll have to be more careful from this timepoint on, now that they have conquered.

My dad has a new car, a silver Saturn, and is proudly explaining its features to me as he turns right instead of left out of Bayliss's eucalyptus-lined driveway.

"Oh, Ernest, pay attention to what you're doing," says my mother from the back seat. She has insisted I sit in front with my father. "You're going the wrong way."

"I know what I'm doing," he asserts, ricocheting a glance off the rear view mirror.

I watch the landscape. I roll the window down at first, longing for the feel of the cool vernal breeze on my face after my month in stasis at Bayliss. But Mom, reminding me of her spring allergies, has me roll it up again. I content myself with peering through the glass at passing semi-rural sights: roadside prickly pear and poisonous oleander, orchards of citrus and avocado, the ubiquitous eucalyptus, fleetingly green pastures with grazing cattle and horses, country cabins, trailer parks, real estate signs, and suburbs looming always over the distant crests of boulder-studded hills. I resist scanning the hillsides and hollows for the shimmering pools of polarized fluorescence I used to observe in my more visionary days. I must try to see only what others see. I have to practice normality.

Bayliss Health Retreat—it sounds like a fat farm instead of a mental hospital—is hidden in one of the many hilly valleys just outside Escondido, in northern San Diego County, tucked away under the philosophy "out of mind, out of sight." After fifteen minutes of winding along narrow backcountry roads, we hit a broad suburban thoroughfare that carries us right to Interstate 15. Thereafter the freeway corridor is polluted by pullulating communities of beige stucco and terra cotta tile roofs, of lockstep condos and office parks, as alike as patches in a Petri dish.

For most of the journey my dad talks to me, my mom making additions and emendations from the back seat when she isn't warning him to slow down. As the rugged, arid hills and valleys of North County—tortured by time, weather, and real estate development—give way to the suburban mesas of San Diego proper, my parents bring me up to date on my grandmother, who at ninety-five has shriveled away to a dry, feeble heap of papery skin and brittle bone. Her mind and memory have likewise withered; she literally cannot tell day from night, and more than once—Dad complains—has called from the seniors home at four in the morning to find out if they are picking her up for dinner.

"I'm going to have her goddamn phone taken out," he adds.

Grandma can no longer keep the names of family members straight, and frequently confuses mother and daughter, father and son, even unto the second and third generation. She no longer has any control of bowels or bladder, so they can't take her anywhere and are loath to have her sitting incontinently around the house. She is going to run out of money this year, my dad claims, and then they don't know what they are going to do with her.

She serves as a terrible reminder of the consequences of living a long and healthy life.

As I listen, I stare into the wide screen of the windshield, watching the gray road unfold in front of us. Freeways braid and unbraid around the 15-163 split, and I think of timespace with its fractal branches and interlooping tendrils. I reflect on being a long pink worm arising from the womb of the woman sitting behind me, my world line growing and stretching through the dimensions, up and down the Pacific coast, across the country, and in epicycloids across the near-vacuum of space as the earth swings around the sun, and the sun around the galaxy. Gazing out of the side window at the marred mesa of Miramar, my reflections reach back to details of my life, picking them up off of dusty storage shelves in the back room of my mental museum, examining them, putting them down again.

I have seen so much over the past decades: the nuclear war that so few noticed, the interwoven realities and probability curves of the rest of the sixties. Later I walked and talked in Better Earth. I watched my life and hopes unravel when the Gateway slipped into the sea, carrying the love of my life with it. Nearly alone I witnessed the invasion of the alien parasites, foreshadowing the umbral Millenium. Almost alone I know the paths not chosen, the futures unrealized, and now the horror ahead.

When my eyes focus again, they settle on my reflection in the window glass, hovering still and ghostly before the speeding detritus of civilization. I see the transparent face of a man past the prime of life, with glossy glasses and a graying mustache. My dad's voice still resonates in the background; he is talking about my sisters now, though I have ceased paying attention.

I know we approach Tierrasanta when I spot the faint khaki cloud that spirals slowly over the neighborhood just east of the freeway. The flat, nebulous spiral recalls the ordnance range that lies beneath Tierrasanta, a relic of World War II. It is also a cyclone of synchronicity, an outward and visible sign of my psychic interface with the invisible. As such I will it away, to avoid an interference pattern with the consensuum. I focus on the road until the spiral becomes mere spin in my peripheral vision, without mass or color. When I dare to look again toward the brown hills, I see only the dull, potato-shaped spots created by tired eyes, and a couple of large, dark birds—ravens or vultures—lazily revolving in its place.

We leave the freeway for a broad suburban thoroughfare, roll east between ranks of eucalyptus, and careen into a warren of ranch houses built in the 1970s. Tierrasanta is a packed neighborhood of wall-to-wall houses, all impeccably maintained stucco and brick, roofed with flammable wood shingle or fire-safe terra cotta tile, landscaped with golf-green lawns and ornamental exotics. There is ample evidence of human life, though I see no one out-of-doors. Turning from Calle del Camino onto Via de la Vuelta, we reach my parents' home, the tidy terminus of their American dream.

"I got your old room ready," my mother announces. The automatic garage door lifts to admit us, and I suppress the feeling of being swallowed as my dad rolls us inside. When we exit the Saturn, Mom faces the cardboard cartons stacked against the back wall. The smell of dust, must, and exhaust fills my nostrils.

"Here's the stuff from your storage, Mike," she says. "I hope this is everything you wanted."

I peruse the unmarked cartons. This is not everything I wanted, but it is all I have.

"Thanks," I mumble, as my dad opens the door to the house.

Somewhere in those boxes, buried in their archeological strata, is the evidence—the photos, the records, the datagem—from Better Earth. And underneath it all, the foundation: the diary of the war that even I forgot. I came to the decision at Bayliss: it is time to spill my story. One last hard look at my memories, the act of dumping them into print, might purge them from my system. Then I can stop looking backward. After all, I turn forty-five this year and have little time left to salvage something of my life. I have to stop looking too far forward, too. There is no profit in being a prophet—not now, here. This manuscript will serve as my testament, my gospel, the bad news, whether anyone reads it or not. It will tell the truth, and nothing but the truth.

It's not my fault it sounds crazy.

Full of Grace

Lenny Lianne

Me, I knew I'd never be cut out
to be a movie-star glamour queen
like Elizabeth Taylor of my paper dolls

so I vowed to grow up to be a nun
during the day and ballerina at night
when I was in Catholic first grade.

To be attired in an ankle-length
outfit, even one so formless,
with the window of my face framed

by a white wimple while sunshine
slanted into classroom number 4
as if straight down from heaven itself,

making me as luminous as the angels
or saints on the holy cards I'd hand out
to eager learners who looked up to me

as bride of Christ and source of wisdom,
well, that was pretty impressive stuff
but undoubtedly just a day job.

So I fancied I'd dance at night
dressed in profuse layers of pale tulle,
one of the beauties in a corps de ballet.

Nightly, I'd wear pink rouge and lipstick,
powder my face, neck and shoulders
and put my beautiful hair in a bun.

Maybe all I wanted in those days
when I couldn't even skip rope
with any skill and was self-conscious

was to be both beautiful and blessed
so I clung to what I understood
as those ambitions most full of grace.

Listeners as the Photo is Taken

Kathleen Elliott Gilroy

The animals are listening:
One horse with the left ear kilted forward—
A foreground horse, just behind the taut wire fence,
eavesdropping intently.

In the far back, one horse with his head
bowed slightly forward; almost imperceptibly—

now, then, the dogs—so open in their purpose,
their attentiveness, their calm energy of communication
and acceptance of these three humans being
        photographed;

true personas open for this moment
when such things are captured by listening hearts
of animals—who do not conceal themselves

with mankind's usual need for wearing alternate faces
to protect themselves from other humans—
who might, by false intent,
enter into sacred, secret-identity, spirit space.

Passing

Steve Montgomery

"Our team or yours?" Roberta nods at a brooding brunette with shaggy locks and a misshapen goatee.

"Bad grooming. He's yours." Val merely glances at the boy coming down the aisle. It's Val's style. He doesn't speak, he makes pronouncements. He can dismiss you with the arch of an eyebrow. And everyone knows his gaydar is impeccable.

To pass the time, the five of us are playing "Whose Team Is He On?" It seems a particularly appropriate game in light of the circumstances. The rules are simple: scan the crowd and guess which boys are straight and which boys are not. Roberta and Toni want to believe that all the cute ones are on their team, while I hold out a desperate hope that at least one of them is not. Val is dispassionate, eliminating hope from the equation. This makes him more accurate than the rest of us. Rocky just sits there looking beautiful.

It is fall, 1978. We are sitting in the front row of a small theatre in the student union building, waiting for David Kopay. Roberta nervously fingers the jacket of his book, *The David Kopay Story*, which has been passed around so much that the edges are already worn. Rocky bought it a few months ago at a bookstore in Salt Lake City—he being the only football fan among us—and read it in one sitting. One by one, each of us devoured it, captivated by the story of the first professional athlete in America to publicly come out of the closet.

And now David Kopay is about to come out of the wings and onto the stage in front of us. Toni saw the notice in the school newspaper, the Idaho State University *Bengal*, and she called me immediately.

"I mean I had to read it twice! Can you believe that ISU had the balls to bring him to Bigotello?" That's what she called our town; she was always telling anyone who would listen that Pocatello had the distinction of being "America's most bigoted city." She couldn't stand the LDS church, and would practically knock missionaries off their bikes in order to tell them what she thought of their beliefs—particularly when it came to women and gays.

"Damn! The Mormons are gonna be *pissed*!" She sounds absolutely gleeful.

I hang up the phone and start giggling. *I'm going to meet David Kopay!* My mind is racing. What will he say? What will *I* say? More importantly, what will I *wear*? His book features pictures of him in his uniform, and for a long time afterward, my imagination featured pictures of him out of his uniform. But it's not just his good looks that appeal to me, it's what he represents.

I begin rummaging through the boxes stacked in my closet. I know it's there . . . a remnant from junior high. I remember wondering at the time why I'd chosen to save it. At last, under an album of newspaper clippings that Mom has kept as souvenirs, I find it. I unfold the butcher paper poster on my bed. There, in the center, is my number: 60. Underneath, "WAY TO GO STEVE!" There are signatures from all the cheerleaders, and cutesy expressions of congratulations strewn about the thing. At the bottom, "1974-75 PERFECT SEASON. GO YELLOWJACKETS!!!"

"GO! C'MON PUSSIES! NOW! C'MON YOU PUSSIES! GET YOUR ASSES OFF THE GROUND! GO! GO! GO!"

Coach Otto's voice assaults every ache in my body, as if he is the master of a voice-operated torture device that implants malevolent clamps designed to squeeze every muscle I possess. I am going to pass out. I know, with certainty, that I am going to pass out. Only fear keeps me conscious.

I feel a giant hand on the small of my back. The hand grabs and twists the waistbands of my athletic shorts and jock, twists them so hard that they become a vice in my crotch. I feel my eyes water. The hand yanks and my legs are airborne. I know what I am supposed to do. I begin crawling forward, using my forearms to propel me across the grass. I am a human wheelbarrow, sagging with fatigue. I wonder how I am able to put one arm in front of the other. I feel the dry Idaho sun on my neck. My body is soaked in sweat. Someone is shouting in my left ear. "You are such a pansy, Montgomery. C'mon crybaby! You want yer mommy? MOVE IT!" The hand lets go and I collapse on the fifty-yard line. The hand's owner steps over me and heads toward his next victim. Through blurry eyes, I see Coach Palmer's wide ass and hairy legs moving down the field. He spits Copenhagen every few yards.

Palmer is a defensive coach and one of the most offensive adults I have ever encountered. He taught me that I am capable of hate. Palmer brings out the Scorpio in me. I fantasize about revenge. The more he humiliates me, the more elaborate my fantasies become. I imagine strapping him to a blocking dummy and letting the entire defensive line pummel him for hours. I picture myself collecting cups of brown spit from all the chew-boys, and forcing Palmer to take a bath in Copenhagen. Best of all is the one where I get to scream obscenities at him while he suffers the agony of Yellow Jacket Road; in my fantasy he is always naked, causing him to earn grass burns in tender places.

It is a sweltering day in late August 1974. For reasons I still cannot fully explain, I have decided to join the football team. We are the Alameda Yellow Jackets. It is week four of our summer practices, and I do not understand why I am still alive.

Yellow Jacket Road is the invention of our head coach, Dick Otto (a name ripe for junior high humor), and he is always telling us that he designed The Road with one goal in mind: peak conditioning. Coach Otto always talks about conditioning, but he never seems to notice what condition I'm in. I am what is called a third-stringer, the name they give to those of us the school makes them keep on the team, despite our total ineptitude on the field. It's the '70s and the school is all about improving our self-esteem; no one is turned away. I am convinced that Coach Otto is sickened by the sight of me. He knows what I am, and it is only now, after years of therapy, that I understand who he was and why I made him squirm.

On this hot August day, however, I am only aware of his disdain. Otto barely speaks to third-stringers. I am certain that he instructs his assistant coaches to make us so miserable that we quit the team. I am determined not to quit—I just don't understand why.

What I dread more than anything else is Yellow Jacket Road. We are divided into small groups along the fifty-yard line, stretching from one side of the field to the other. For what seems like an eternity, but is really only ninety minutes, the coaches put us through a series of drills that I can only describe as physical and mental torture—worse than being forced to watch a Joan Rivers marathon while actually running a marathon. Every drill requires us to move up five yards, back five yards, up ten yards, back ten yards—and so on, until we have run half the length of the field and back. At first we do basic sprints, forward, backward, sideways—one foot crossing over the other in a scissors pattern. But then we crawl on our hands and knees, or pull ourselves along by our forearms, dragging our legs behind us, or waddle like ducks until our legs feel like goal posts beneath us.

The physical pain is excruciating enough. Even more painful is the constant humiliation. Apparently, the coaches feel that the worst insults they can spew at us are the ones that liken us to women or homosexuals. Favorite invectives of the first order include "girls" and "ladies," as in, "C'mon ladies, we're not puttin' on a goddamn fashion show. Put away yer girlie makeup and start playin' some FOOTBALL!"

When it comes to the other category, each coach seems to have his favorite expression. Coach Otto's word of choice is "pussy" ("Yer all a bunch of pussies! That's what ya are! Pussy-boys!"), while Coach Palmer prefers "pansy" ("Montgomery, yer nothin' but a goddamn pansy!"). Coach Little, the lead offensive coach, is partial to "fairy," usually accompanied by an exaggerated mince-dance and what are still the limpest wrists I've ever seen (and believe me, I've seen plenty). Whenever he does this, I run a mini-movie in my head: the coaches are all at Otto's house drinking beer and watching Monday night football; their halftime entertainment features Coach Little doing his Little Dance over and over and over, like a deranged monkey. It helps me get through practice.

"SHOWERS!" That thrilling word. That line of demarcation: practice is over. I have survived one more day. I feel a surge of energy, and I spring to my feet. I am surprised at my body's ability to do anything. Moments before, I was incapable of movement. Now, I am running across the field. It is the promise of the locker room, the cool-hot water, permission to laugh, the absence of order. Boys allowed to be boys once again.

Still, I am out of my element. This is the wide world of sports and I have managed only a narrow point of entry. I am not a flipper of towels or a grabber of genitals. In the locker room, I become an anthropologist. I study them—their unstudied movements, the jocular cadence of their speech, the way they put on underwear. These are the boys my father conjured during those joyous nine months of waiting, anticipating, longing. I was not in the picture.

So I must learn the things that they know through instinct. Every moment I am in their presence is an act of discovery. My own fear of being discovered makes me uncharacteristically silent. The less I say, the more they will think I am one of them. Passing has become my pastime. It will be many years before I grasp the toll that passing requires.

I am certain that it is my eyes that give me away. I cannot help but stare. I am surrounded by physical beauty made even more potent because I have earned the right to be there. Perhaps that is what propels me to follow the Yellow Jacket Road to its grueling conclusion. I may not be able to throw a ball or tackle an opponent, but I have not given up and that should stand for something.

I reward myself with furtive glances. There is the sheer bulk of Karl Donaldson, taller and wider than every other boy, his muscles honed moving irrigation pipe in the summer and harvesting potatoes in the fall. I am fascinated with the hair that covers every inch of Vince Farrelli. At sixteen—he's been "held back" twice—he has more body hair than anyone I've ever seen. Since I am practically hairless, to my eyes Vince is part movie-star-sex-symbol, part can't-turn-away-from-it circus freak. There is the fullness of Brett Ray's jockstrap, Lonnie King's ultra-broad shoulders, and the way Bobby Robertson's pale skin glistens when he's wet.

But my favorite is Randy Ford. He is perfect. Long brown hair that sticks to his neck when he sweats. Wide brown eyes with lashes you just want to lick. A mouth that pouts even when he smiles. And a body any sculptor would be proud to claim. Lately, I find myself conserving glances for him. I have worked out an elaborate algorithm in my head, and each day allot myself so many "secret looks." My daily allotment tends to go up according to the misery level of that day's practice. The more I'm around Randy, the less I want to look at the others. I am so nervous around him that I can barely say hello, and I am constantly in fear that he will catch me staring at him. I am both embarrassed and exhilarated by my own boldness.

"What're you lookin' at faggot?" I am frozen. My ears begin to burn and I imagine that my face is as red as Zeke Miller's hair.

There is a scuffle behind me. I turn around to find Ricky Culpepper on the ground, his hands over his face, kicking his legs in self-defense. Brett Ray is standing over him, fist poised, shouting a string of obscenities. It is not the first time Brett has reacted this way. I have managed to fly beneath his radar, but others have not been so lucky. Especially Ricky, with his delicate features and high voice. Ricky doesn't even try to pass.

I'm relieved that it's not me, but I am ashamed at my relief. I'd like to record here that I stood up for Ricky, that I fought the good fight—but I cannot. On that day, Ricky was camouflage, and I was chameleon. Every pansy for himself.

Ricky was gone long before we played our first game. His family moved to Nampa, and I moved up on the radar screen. But somehow I managed to claim membership on our "perfect season" team, although I don't recall playing in a single game. If I did, it is now just a blur of missed opportunities. I played positions that I am still unable to describe in any detail: center and nose guard. I was clearly left of center, and like Cyrano, the only nose worth guarding was my own.

The poster appeared in my bedroom a week after our season ended. It felt strange, knowing that a group of giggling girls had invaded my inner sanctum while I was away. Dad let them in while I ate ice cream with Randy Ford—okay, with the whole team—at 39 Flavors; a final treat from our sadistic coaches. Dad couldn't wait to follow me to my room, to see my reaction to the balloons and streamers and the giant poster on the wall. Celebration of a sports hero—it was the closest we would come to living out his dream.

The theater is only half full as David Kopay walks out onto the stage and begins to tell his story. He is older than I imagined—I realize that all the snapshots I've frozen in my brain are of him in his early twenties, playing college ball. He is now thirty-six; I am seventeen. I secretly want him to be more virile—if we're gonna have an icon, the butch-er the better.

Since we have all read his book, the story is familiar. Kopay excelled at passing. He was a man's man, even getting married to prove his total commitment to the game. Had we been contemporaries, he would have been included in my ration of stolen glances. It makes me wonder who my team's Kopay might have been. My money was on Brett Ray, his explosive anger toward Ricky a consequence of unresolved skirmishes within.

Kopay is at a small table signing copies of his book. As we wait in line, we dare Roberta to ask him to join us for a drink. She does, and we are astounded when he accepts. In less than an hour, we find ourselves having cocktails with David Kopay. I am underage, but no one seems to care. I am excited by his celebrity, although he goes unrecognized by the other patrons. For some reason, we have chosen a straight bar rather than going to Bernie's. Was it his choice? Ours?

What begins as a group conversation soon deteriorates. Kopay cannot take his eyes off of Rocky, the one straight man at the table. He has pulled his chair closer to Rocky's, and every inch of his body language communicates intense desire. Their conversation becomes so exclusive that the rest of us display our dismay openly, exchanging obscene gestures and barbed remarks. We know he cannot hear us, so deeply engrossed is he in his own charisma. When he has the chance, Rocky gives us a pleading look that says, "Save me!"

Roberta loudly reminds everyone at the table that we have early-morning classes. On cue, we suck down our drinks, tip the waitress, and head for the door. We wait for Rocky outside, allowing him to turn Kopay down in private. They emerge together, and our celebrity guest clearly isn't taking "no" for an answer. Rocky practically has to push him away from the door of Roberta's Celica, so that she can drive away.

Later, at Roberta's apartment, Rocky fills us in on the sordid details. It seems Mr. Kopay offered Rocky quite a menu of sexual options, including things we had only read about in dirty magazines. We spent the night laughing about our adventures, and having bawdy fun at Rocky's expense. In the course of a few hours, an idol had fallen, reclaiming his human status once again.

Maybe I am not the only one clinging to imperfect memories of untouchable boys, longing to be what we are not. Maybe some of us were never meant to pass.

"The tulips should be behind bars like dangerous animals."
—Sylvia Plath

My Tulips' Interment

Sydney Brown

The tulips have opened and they are red.
I have written this because I said it to my husband
ten minutes ago without meaning it to be anything
more than an observation on some flowers we picked
up at the farmers' market last Friday.

Years ago
my first thought would have been Sylvia,
how the tulips' redness in a white room
next to her medical chart,
next to her overnight bag,
beside the photo of her children
offended her quest for quiet still.

Last week we considered ways to cut
costs in light of recent gasoline prices,
and my level-headed husband,
his nails manicured backyard brown,
suggested we stop using fabric softener
and I responded, "Never—
I have grown accustomed to fabric softener."

Most of life is this way;
    we grow accustomed to what we do not need
    as we grow farther away from what we do.

When the tulips die, I pour their water
on a hearty rose bush in the backyard,
then place their still-barbed little bodies
in a green recycling bin,
next to a blue recycling bin,
next to a colossal gray trash bin
beside the air conditioning unit
pumping sweet coolness into our home,
the drone of its work
the dirge of my tulips' interment.

Aqbat Jaber

Chris Baron

Refugee camp, Jericho, West Bank, Israel

Black flags rise above open ceilings
mourning the death of Saddam Hussein
and the streets are not streets
just dirt paths dust really inside my lungs
Suliman teaches me to say *marhaba*
welcomes me with this rounded word
asks me to use it as a greeting
and so I say it over and over to everyone I see
marhaba to the shy girl in the doorway with no building
marhaba to the Bedouin father
who invites us for chalky tea
and an afternoon bathed in blue smoke
marhaba to the mother who pulls her daughter closer in
marhaba to the goats
to the group of young men
sons of Palestine
who reach into themselves
pull out their toughness
wear it like a necklace
only the chain is rusted and broken
and I feel more sad than afraid
marhaba to the young children
who clamor over my camera
hold up peace signs
make scary faces and the little girls
who shy away laughing, running away
over and over
marhaba to Ahmed
round as his soccer ball in his blue-hooded sweatshirt
of *Che*, looking tough even in the West Bank
marhaba from the depths of me
to the men at the mosque
with wisdom breath
and skin held together
by strife

One of These Nights

Steve Montgomery

"You don't want to be a goody-two-shoes your whole life, do ya?"

Dee Woods knows how to get to me.

"C'mon, Steve, don't be a wuss. Try it."

Dee may not be the swiftest raft on the rapids, but he has what his mother calls "figure-it-out smarts." At the moment, Dee is figuring out how I work.

"No. I'm not going to, I told you—no big deal."

"How do you know you're not gonna like it if you don't try it at least once?"

Now he's appealing to my crippling sense of logic. He knows he's getting to me. I try again.

"I don't have to jump into the Portneuf in January to know that it's cold as hell—I just know."

"Yeah, but whose askin' you to jump into the Portneuf?" Dee counters, "I just want you to take a toke off this joint. Everybody here's smokin' out 'cept you."

Now appealing to my budding rebelliousness, and my insatiable need to be accepted by others. He's good, I'll give him that. He also has me pinned into a corner—literally, his knee between my legs implying a very real threat of groin damage—on the floor of the bathroom in the single-wide trailer he shares with his mother, sister, and kid brother Charlie.

Charlie is the only reason I'm even there. Ever since he'd begun making appearances in my fourteen-year-old dreams, I'd been doing just about anything to be near Charlie Woods.

"Look, I'm drunk. I've been drinkin' outta the keg all night," I protest as I try unsuccessfully to un-wedge myself from the space between the toilet and his mom's lime green vanity. Even drunk, I'm punching my logic card—after all, goody-two-shoes don't get drunk, everybody knows that. This is the summer of my discontent, and I want credit for the work I've done to undo my good-little-boy image.

"Beer. Big deal. Wait'll ya try this stuff. Beer'll seem like warm piss. Don't be a pussy." Dee knows how much I hate that name—that I might just do anything to prove him wrong. It's the name I heard all last summer from Coach Otto as he humiliated me for my failed attempts at being a football player.

Dee stares into me with those glassy green eyes, his long, wiry brown hair pushing down on drooping eyelids. Dee and Dream-Boy both hate their hair, and spend a lot of time trying to uncrimp the native waves they inherited from their sad and beautiful half-Cherokee mother. Dee's hair is coarse and unkempt. Charlie's is soft as silk, and I love the way it looks damp with reservoir water on the way home from our American Falls swimming trips. I want to run my fingers through it, want to feel it brush against me as I kiss those full sax-player lips.

I am thinking of Charlie's lips as his brother's lips come in closer, pucker, and begin blowing smoke into my eyes. I hold my breath, not wanting to inhale any of it. But as he shoves the joint up to my mouth I give in. I invite my first lungful of marijuana, knowing with certainty that I am now damned forever. This is the line I said I would never cross. It was one thing to concoct suicide drinks with Charlie, filching alcohol from my parents' liquor bottles, but it was quite another to smoke pot. That was the slippery slope we'd heard about when we went to that assembly in the gym last year. First it was drinking, now pot; next stop heroin.

It was also one more secret I had to keep.

Dee is giddy with triumph. He climbs off me shouting, "Montgomery's a stoner! Montgomery's a stoner!" as he returns to the living room to join his friends. I'm mortified. Will someone tell my parents? Is everyone at school going to find out in the fall?

Charlie appears in the bathroom doorway, laughing. He puts his hand out to help pull me up. I am touched by the gesture. Maybe now he'll see I'm cool enough for him to hang out with me even more. Although we're both fourteen, Charlie will still be at Alameda in the fall—consequence of Mom's decision to start me in the first grade when I was five. I think about how much I will miss sitting next to him in band class, feeling his shoulder pressing up against mine when we play. Although it is only June,

I am already worried that our summer together will pass too quickly.

We get another beer and plop down on the floor next to the stereo. It is one of those consoles built to blend in with the living room furniture. The top has two wood panels that slide open; one side is for storing records, and the other side has a built-in turntable. Dee's playing his new Eagles album.

"Your brother must have this on Replay—this is about the tenth time I've heard this song!" When Charlie and I hang out together, I'm always the talker. Charlie never says much, especially when he's stoned. Tonight, I feel like I don't want to stop talking. I want to talk about everything. More than anything, I want to tell Charlie how I feel about him. But my fear is even more powerful than the pot.

Someone passes Charlie a joint. After a long toke, he passes it to me. I imagine that it is only his saliva I feel as I press my lips against the moist Zig-Zag paper. I want to continue passing it back and forth between us, exchanging paper kisses, but there is another thumb and forefinger poised in my periphery, so I pass the joint along.

I thought by nowwwww you'd realiiiiiize / There ain't no way to hide your lyin' eyes.

Suddenly, through the magic of marijuana, the Eagles are singing about me. Every line of the song now has *meaning.* Does Charlie know that *my* smile is a "thin disguise" for the way I really feel about him. Does he realize that *he* is the boy with the "fiery eyes"? Does he understand why, in band class, I never pull away when his leg accidentally touches mine? I want the song to play over and over and over until Charlie finally gets the message. Then he'll stand up, extend his hand to me, and pull me into his arms and out of my longing.

A few weeks after Dee's party, Charlie and I are at my house making suicides. Charlie knows how to drain minute quantities from each bottle and then replace the missing liquor with water. So far it's worked, but I'm in constant fear of getting caught.

We clink our blue Tupperware glasses, plug our noses and guzzle. I feel a slow burn in my chest and my arms break out in goose bumps. The concoction is disgusting. An involuntary horse whinny escapes from my mouth and nose. Charlie never shows a reaction. He considers it a weakness.

"I wish we could get your brother's friend to buy us some more Boone's Farm or MD 20/20—at least those taste sweet." It doesn't take much hard liquor to get me drunk. Charlie, who can drink half a bottle of vodka and still function in the world, once joked, "Steve, you're not just a lightweight, you're a featherweight." It was meant to be derogatory. Variation on a theme—pussy, fag, wuss, wimp, featherweight. The nicknames of my youth.

Charlie just smiles at me. He's happy to have a summer drinking buddy. I'm just happy to see Charlie smile. When he's not drinking, Charlie seldom smiles. He has a chipped front tooth that embarrasses him. Even when he's drunk, I often see him bring the back of his hand over his mouth when he laughs. But sometimes he forgets and his laugh is radiant.

We decide to ride our bikes over to Tina Singer's house. Tina has a pool—a rarity in Pocatello—and she lets us swim there while her parents are at work. I start to feel the buzz as we throw our bikes on Tina's front lawn. I stumble over my rear tire and fall. Charlie thinks this is hilarious. I laugh it off, ignoring the grass burn on my right knee. Tina is already sunning herself by the pool. She is taller than I am, with knobby knees and lanky legs poking out of an ill-fitting pair of boy's swim trunks. Her bikini top seems unnecessary; she is as flat-chested as we are.

I watch as Charlie casually pulls his tank top up and over his head, revealing his remarkable chest and stomach. I have just moved out of my "Sears husky" phase, so I am envious of his naturally toned muscles. He is also as brown as I am white. That Cherokee blood. I have only blonde blood. Norwegians and Germans and Danes (oh my!).

As we splash and dive and wrestle the afternoon away in Tina's pool, I am aware—as I always am when I'm with Charlie— that I experience the events of this ordinary summer day as two boys in one. Surface Boy is the carefree buddy pallin' around with his friend Charlie. Everything's cool. Life is a gas. What, me worry?

Beneath the surface, chaos reigns. Miss Carlisle once conducted an experiment in class to demonstrate that the speed of sound in water is about five times faster than the speed of sound in air. The part of me that exists beneath the surface is inundated by the sounds of self-doubt, sexual desire and, most of all, shame. And like whales and dolphins, I have developed a sophisticated language for use down there. The language of submersion. It allows me to tell Charlie all the things I feel for him in symbols he cannot yet decode.

As we are pedaling away from Tina's house, Charlie suggests a sleepover at my house. "I might have a surprise that'll put us both in a good mood." I'm guessing he's going to try to steal a joint from his brother's stash.

That night, we listen to Elton John records in my bedroom and talk about school and the new bikes we want for our birthdays. Once we are sure my parents are in bed, we grab our sleeping bags and head for the back yard. Charlie says we should be as close to the alley as possible.

Then he tells me about his surprise.

". . . so I told them to meet us at the swings at Alameda Park at midnight. This'll be really cool, Steve."

It turns out Charlie has invited Becky and Theresa, two girls we know from junior high, to participate in a midnight rendezvous that Charlie hopes will lead to sex. I am petrified. And a little bit angry with Charlie. Why would he do this? I have no interest in meeting a couple of skanky girls at the park, but I can't let Charlie know how I feel. So I go along with the plan.

A little before twelve we put our pillows in our sleeping bags, just in case my father looks out the back window while we're gone, then slip down the alley and across the street to the park.

After forty-five minutes of playing on the swings and teeter-totters, it is clear that the girls are a no-show. Charlie is disappointed. I am relieved. We head back to my house and, to my double relief, the lights are off.

As we settle into our sleeping bags, Charlie tells me that he was really hoping the girls would show because the whole thing has him "horny as hell." On the surface, I am silent. I notice that my heart is beating faster. I am grateful for the darkness so that Charlie cannot see how flushed I am.

What he says next takes me completely by surprise.

"We could always do the next best thing."

All I can think of to say is, "What's *that*?"—knowing full well what *that* is.

I feel all those submerged voices rising to the surface. They are shouting one moment, whispering the next. Eagles songs and Elton songs compete for my attention. Desperados and Brown Dirt Cowboys stirring up dust storms in my head. I wonder if I am dreaming and suddenly feel terror at the prospect of waking.

But tangible things seem to be happening. Through the storm in my head, I hear Charlie telling me to unzip my sleeping bag and lay it out flat on the grass. He is already unzipping his to use as a blanket that will keep us warm—and keep our encounter under cover.

As we begin, the only surface words spoken consist of Charlie warning me that if I tell anyone he'll beat the shit out of me, and me telling Charlie that I would never tell a soul. After all, I've learned plenty of ways to hide eyes that tell lies.

I wait for Charlie to start. His touch is softer than I imagined it would be. His hands move slowly along my chest. Afraid to do anything Charlie might not want to do, I begin to mirror his movements, my touch merely a reflection of his. At one point, I feel his elbow digging into the grass burn I earned on Tina's front lawn. I want to tell him to readjust, but I am afraid of disturbing the precarious equilibrium that exists now that we are undercover. This is the world I know best—submersion and subversion. I fear the sound of my voice will force our ascent to the surface of this sub-aqua world, where we will find ourselves gasping for words that were once unnecessary. I want us to remain wordless, flooded by the sensual, my intellect dormant for once.

Like a still lake stirred by the pulse of a pebble, my entire body ripples with each touch—even those that sting. So I give in to the pain. Small price to pay for such intense pleasure.

There would be many more encounters after that night, usually when Charlie was drunk or stoned so he could pretend not to remember what happened. Michael, a character in *The Boys in the Band*, calls it the "Christ-was-I-drunk-last-night syndrome." It allows boys who think of themselves as straight to avoid coming face-to-face with their same-sex trysts.

Soon after that night in my back yard, I saw what happened to anyone who dared speak about Charlie's unspeakable acts. Charlie and I had ridden our bikes to A&W drive-in, one of our favorite obstacle courses. We were popping wheelies and trying out new tricks when Charlie's friend Sam showed up. Sam and Charlie had lived next to each other since birth, and Charlie had clearly established himself as the alpha dog, making fun of just about everything that came out of Sam's mouth. Sam would try various retorts, but Charlie always won. I didn't care much for Sam, so I just laughed along with Charlie and his barrage of insults.

But that day was different. Charlie was being particularly harsh, berating Sam for his ugly freckles and low IQ.

"The only woman you'll ever get will be a filthy hooker with VD."

I'm not sure if Sam's response came more from anger or desperation, but it enraged Charlie.

"Yeah, well maybe I'll tell Steve about the kind of women *you* like."

I knew immediately what Sam meant. Sam and Charlie had done the next best thing, and Sam was threatening to tell.

The words were barely out of Sam's mouth when I saw Charlie lean forward on his bike and aim his front tire directly at Sam. The collision threw Sam against the pavement and Charlie was on him in an instant, pummeling his fists against Sam's upraised hands, securing several blows to his face and chest.

"Shut up you fuckhead. Fucker. I'm gonna fuckin' kill you."

Charlie's face was fury red as he stood up and began kicking Sam in the back. Sam was curled up, crying for Charlie to stop. To my surprise, he did stop. Then he picked up Sam's bike and hurled it over his head. It crashed and skidded across the parking lot, and without a word Charlie got on his bike and rode away. Sam was already scurrying toward his own bike, afraid of Charlie's return. I just stood there stunned.

Charlie and I never once spoke about that day, but the message was clear. Like the barbarian who mounts severed heads on stakes at the entrance to his village, Charlie had shown me that there were consequences for revealing his secret.

Over the next year or so, Charlie's machismo grew in direct proportion to the number of times we fooled around. I always knew I was the *next* best thing. I was never chosen first. That privilege belonged to the many girls Charlie lusted over in my presence.

"Look at *her*, Steve. Man, I'd like to taste some of *that*."

But when he couldn't taste some of that, Charlie knew that he could count on me to satisfy his hunger. My desire to be with him was far stronger than the hurt I felt at being the choice of last resort. I knew that if I wanted to be with Charlie, pleasure would forever be coupled with pain.

When Charlie finally ended it, he did so with angry force. I know now that it wasn't me at the source of his anger. His fears, it turns out, were even more powerful than mine. But at the time, I didn't understand any of it. I wondered what I'd done wrong, how I could have been more of what he wanted me to be. Hadn't I done everything he'd asked of me? I'd crossed lines that had once been uncrossable, just to hear him call me his friend.

For once, I had nothing more to give.

old guy

Gary Winters

I've been on a quest to reinvent myself as an old guy. It hasn't been going too well. Not at all really. Because the more I come to grips with this new self-image the younger I feel. I'm seeing all sorts of things for the first time. Things that were always there but I sped past them on my way somewhere. My mind's in a constant state of blown away. One hell of a way to be an old guy.

Ars Poetica

Una Nichols Hynum

Churning butter, I turn the handle
of the Mason jar until my arm
gets tired. I rest and crank again.
The unexpectedness

of what happens is like coming
upon an acre of wild daisies.
Out of thick, white cream,
clusters of yellow cling to beaters.

I pour off the whey, place
nuggets of butter on a plate,
pat and smooth, working out
the grey droplets. Finished,

I lower the dazzling mound
into the artesian coolness
of a well, careful not to break
the plate against the stone.

Just Passing Through

Dave Riessen

Karl and I were up at Crazy Eddie's doing jumps off of Eat Your Lunch when we first saw the storm coming in. The day had been hot, in the nineties, and very few, if any, clouds were overhead. It was late afternoon, about an hour before dinner, when we first heard the distant rumble of thunder.

Crazy Eddie walked down from his house and joined us, sipping on his beer, watching the clouds. Then he turned and pointed to a pole he had mounted on the other side of his house, further up the hill, the top of which was higher than his roof by about twenty feet.

"That ain't no flagpole," he said, rubbing his hand over the stubble of his beard. "No siree. Ball o' lightnin' came through my house last summer, sizzlin' and cracklin', lookin' like a ball o' brains on fire."

Both Karl and I laughed.

"Thought I was ha-loo-cin-a-tin," he said.

"Where'd it go?" I asked.

"Say, what?"

"The ball of lightning, where did it go?"

"Wherever it wanted," said Crazy Eddie, grinning. "No way I'm touchin' it."

"It must've gone someplace," I said. "Maybe out a window?"

"Burnt a hole through my cupboard door, found a water pipe."

"Where'd it come from?" said Karl.

"Say, what?"

"Lightning. How'd it get in?"

"I had this antennie, for my ray-dee-yo, I was listenin' for news 'bout the storm. Damn thing blew up, sittin' right there on the shelf. Pow! Jest like that. Jesus. I got my news, I'll tell ya."

"Did it float?" I asked. "Or roll?"

"Say, what?"

"The fireball. Was it floating in the air? Or rolling on the floor?"

"Shit, Slick. I'm not sure, come to think of it . . . ."

"Here we go," said Karl. "Don't answer him, Eddie. Next thing, we'll be standing here in the rain doing experiments."

"How fast was it going?" I asked.

"I thinks, slow," said Crazy Eddie. "But I wasn't countin'. You know, time gets mysterious, 'specially when weird shit happens, seems like forever."

"Could you have outrun it?" I asked.

"I'da tried, 'cept it had me trapped in the corner. Shorty says, put me a pole up there on the hill, and that'll 'tract the lightnin'. I calls it Hooker. Work's good, too. You oughtta see all the sparks I get."

Standing at our launch point, I guessed the pole was located about fifty or sixty feet beyond the back of Eddie's house, which was located about two-thirds of the way up on the back of his lot.

"How does the lightning know to hit the pole and not the house?" said Karl.

"Woolsy," said Crazy Eddie, grinning. "Good question, ain't it? That's why I keeps me a storm supply a whiskey, for con-tem-plaa-tion, not Crow, though. I was drinkin' Crow that night. Ain't touched a drop since." He spit. "Cain't trust it."

More thunder. We could see the flashes in the distance, back inside the clouds.

"Coming right at us," said Karl.

"Bout two hours, I reckon," said Crazy Eddie, turning, walking back up the hill. "You got one of them tee-vee's? Reckon I'd unplug the thing. And I wouldn't be leavin' no antennie wire inside my house, neither. Never knows what might come through."

Karl and I rode back into town, following the gravel road until we reached the pavement, then turned on the speed and coasted south down State Street, the same hill we'd sledded last winter. The skies started turning gray. The wind was picking up.

Riding in front, Karl waved good-bye when we reached my house, and continued on. I put my bike up on the porch. I could feel the rain coming, a kind of heavy pressure in the air. Grandma was watching the news when I came through the front door.

"Grandma, I . . ."

She put her finger to her lips. "Shhh."

Senator Ralph Flanders introduced a resolution in the Senate today calling for the censure of Senator Joe McCarthy. "The senator," he said, "has a habitual contempt for people."

"We interrupt this program to warn residents of a severe thunderstorm . . . ."

Mat came out of the bathroom, wiping his hands on his pants rather than using the towel in the bathroom. I motioned for him to follow me out to the front porch, which he did. We sat on the steps, watching a dust devil coming up State Street, bringing with it a napkin or sack, we couldn't tell, spiraling higher than the trees, leaves tumbling along at the bottom, rolling and skittering in a wild, whirling circle across the road.

The first few drops of rain hit the ground hard, causing dust to fly up in little puffs, and the fall was sporadic, hitting here or there, but not yet really coming down. I felt like holding my breath, everything seemed suspended, waiting for the inevitable. But then the rain stopped altogether, and we felt a colder breeze move through.

"Somethin's gonna happen," I said to Mat.

"Yup," said Mat, resting his chin on his hands, elbows on his knees.

Grandma walked down the porch and joined us at the steps, standing at the end of the banister.

"Ready to break," she said, studying the clouds. "Any minute. Why don't you boys come up here." Her voice inflected a statement more than a question.

"We'll be OK," I said.

"Yup," said Mat, nodding.

"I don't think so," said Grandma.

"We're just two little dots," I said, wanting to keep my view of the sky as wide as possible. "What are the chances . . . "

"No arguing."

Suddenly, the sky lit up. I saw the light but, looking up at Grandma, missed the flash. I turned back around, and was surprised to see how dark the clouds had become in just the last minute.

"Ohhh," said Mat, clapping his hands.

Thunder bellowed across the sky in a huge boom, followed by several aftershocks that rattled the windows, lasting several seconds, and ending in a low rumble.

"Uh oh, " said Mat, getting up and joining Grandma on the porch.

Suddenly the rain let loose—large, heavy drops pelting the dry ground like a drum, hitting the roof in hefty thuds, sudden sheets of water heading for the gutters, coming down in a rush, and through the trees, blasting the leaves with a roar that came from everywhere, drenching the town all at once. The argument about sitting on the steps was over. I joined them under the roof.

"When's Dad getting back?" I asked, wiping the drops off of my cheeks.

"Supposed to be here already," said Grandma, looking down State Street toward town.

"He just went to get groceries?"

"If Mitch is working," said Grandma, which he probably was, since the hardware store didn't close until six, "they'll talk all night."

"What's for dinner?"

"Pork chops, if he ever gets here." She turned back toward the front door. "Guess I'll call. Stay up on the porch."

Minutes later, Dad pulled up to the front of the house. By then the rain was coming down so hard that any attempt to get from the car to the house, a distance of about fifty feet, would result in an absolute drenching. Mat and I stood near the front steps, waiting. Dad remained in the car with our uncooked pork chops.

Just when it seemed like the rain could not come down any harder, it did. Walls of water fell from the sky. Sidewalks turned into streams, State Street, a river. Mat and I moved back up against the house, well under the cover of the roof.

I don't know if lightning came down and hit Dad's car on the bumper, or if sparks leaped up from the metal toward the sky, the strike was so instantaneous and continuous. Thunder was instant and seemed like it should have broken the windows. For a split second, the street, the sky, and the bumper of Dad's

1949 Ford coupe, were connected by a glowing snake of light. Mat headed for the front door at a dead run.

I could not imagine why Dad was not hurt by the strike. It seemed like he should have died, but he just looked out through the rain-splattered window and laughed. How could someone survive that, a direct hit? The rain seemed to subside after that, at least long enough for Dad to race from the car to the porch.

Pork chops delivered, and dinner on the way, Dad, Mat and I sat on the front porch, with Grandma popping her head out through the front door from time to time, all of us watching the storm. Lightning flashed. Dad counted.

"Eleven," he said.

"Seconds?" I asked.

"Right. About two miles."

"Five seconds a mile?" I asked, doing the math.

"Right."

"Yup," said Mat, nodding as if he understood.

"How long is a mile?" I asked.

"About five thousand feet, actually, a little more. Five thousand, two hundred and eighty feet."

"So, a thousand feet a second, for sound," I concluded. "How fast is lightning?"

"Don't know about lightning. Light is 186,000 miles per second."

"Per *second*?"

"Pretty fast," said Dad.

"Wow," I said, trying to comprehend that much speed. "How did they measure that?"

"Something about Jupiter and one of its moons, Io," said Dad, pausing for rumbling thunder. "Takes less time for sunlight reflecting off of Io to get to Earth when we are on one side of the sun, closest to Jupiter, than on the other. It just happened to be 186,000."

"When did they discover that?"

"About three hundred years ago, give or take fifty."

"What?"

"Some of those guys were pretty sharp."

"How do you know all of this?"

"I'm a science teacher . . . this year."

"I thought you were the gym coach."

"In the mornings."

"Is that the *exact* speed?"

"One hundred eighty-six thousand, three hundred, eighty-four, I think."

"How'd they figure that out?"

"This guy, Michelson, I think, used mirrors between two mountaintops, twenty-two miles apart, and measured how long it took to get from one mirror to the other, and back again."

I tried to comprehend that as well. It didn't make sense. It would take far, far less than one second for light to go twenty-two miles and come back again, even before you finished pushing the start button. Dad and Mat remained sitting while I paced the porch to mull this over.

The air was warm now, rain coming down more evenly, steady. Night was upon us. Light flashed in the distance. Mat and Dad counted the seconds.

"Twenty-four," said Dad.

"Free," said Mat.

"Twenty-two miles isn't long enough," I said, at last.

"I'll draw it out for you later," said Dad, knowing that I was having trouble with this. "He used an eight-sided rotating mirror."

"What?"

That information didn't help either. I was more confused than ever. "How come lightning doesn't go as fast as light? Aren't they the same thing?"

"Nope," he said, shaking his head. "Lightning is static electricity. Air caught in the spark gets hot, explodes, and creates lightning, which travels at the speed of light."

"But . . . "

"Dinner's ready," said Grandma, sticking her head out the front door.

Another flash, and all the lights went out, not just us, everyone up and down the street. I remembered Crazy Eddie's warning about the antenna and wondered how he was faring.

Grandma lit two candles at the table while I went inside to disconnect the TV, but it had already been done.

"Who undid the TV?" I asked, sitting down at the table.

"I did," said Grandma, dishing buttered potatoes onto my plate.

"How did you know to do that?" I asked.

"I'm not one of God's fools," said Grandma. "Go wash your hands. Take your brother with you."

When we returned to the table, the conversation had moved on. We said grace and ate by candlelight.

"Mitch said Martha Simmons fell down," said Dad. "Broke her hip."

"Don't believe everything Mitch says," said Grandma.

"That's what Abe said. Told Mitch when he came in to buy some bolts, so he could fix her gate."

"They don't know her hip's broken," said Grandma, well aware of the gossip in town.

"I heard she might have to sell the farm," said Dad, buttering a roll. "Ever since Fred died, she's had to pay for more help, can't make a profit."

"Sell it?" said Grandma. "Where would she go?"

"There's this nursing home in Randolf—"

"Randolf!" said Grandma, pausing in the middle of cutting her pork chop. "She doesn't *know* anybody over there."

"Dad," I asked. "How far away is the moon?"

"What?"

"How far away is the moon?"

"Uh . . . about 240,000 miles, I think. Why?"

"Just thinking."

"What's the moon got to do with anything?" asked Grandma.

"Something Dad said. If lightning flashed a mile away from us, people on the moon could see it before we heard it, right?"

"There are no people on the moon," said Grandma.

"But if there were."

"I suppose so," said Dad, doing the math as he chewed.

That ended the conversation about Martha Simmons, not that I was trying to do that. I had finally gotten my grip on the speed of light. I did the math later and discovered that light could go to the moon and back, almost twice, before we heard the sound, if it hit a mile away. The lights came back on. Mat and I blew out the candles.

After dinner, Mat and I retreated to the attic. Dad tucked us in, went back down the stairs, and turned out the lights. Light flashed through our room. Mat and I counted the seconds.

"Fourteen," I said. "Almost three miles."

"Free," said Mat. "Almo free my."

"Yep," I said, liking the sound of the distant thunder, feeling secure under the roof, under my blanket, and listening to the storm. Our conversation ended as we drifted off into our dreams.

Some time later we heard a loud boom, which brought both Mat and I to sitting positions in our beds. I went to the window and peered out. Mat decided that under the covers was a better idea.

Rain was still falling hard, and the wind had picked up, blowing even harder than when we had gone to bed. Looking out through both the windows, I found nothing unusual, and went back to bed.

Sometime in the next ten minutes, a brilliant flash of light burst into our room, thunder arriving at the same time, sounding like a bomb had exploded in the attic. Lightning had hit close, very close. Mat came out from under the covers, heading for the stairs like he was shot from a cannon.

"Mat!" I yelled. "It's OK!"

"Nup," he said, shaking his head, and turning around backwards to descend, the only way he knew how.

"They'll grab your ankles," I said, reminding him of our previous conversations. I wasn't trying to be mean, there was more to it than that.

"Whuts?" Mat asked one night, soon after we had moved in.

Translated, he was asking, "What is it?" And I knew that he was referring to a soft creaking sound that seemed to come out of the woodwork, not just the roof, but the walls, the floor, and sometimes it could even be heard down in the cellar, sounding like two pieces of rusty metal scraping together, a heavy door hinge creaking.

I felt like someone was peeking in from some hidden door when it happened at night, looking to find something of interest, and then coming into the room, or not, with the door creaking a second time, closing. I assumed this because one creak ended with an up note, and the other ended sounding down. The time between opening and closing varied, from just a few seconds, to several minutes, one creak following the other.

That sound was one of the first objects of our attention in the house, which we soon came to realize, was only one of many. The house creaked, moaned, and sometimes windows rattled, seemingly for no reason. The creaking sound almost never occurred in the morning, rarely during the day, and most frequently at night, at about our bedtime.

Mat and I methodically went through the house, floor by floor, and opened and closed every object that had a hinge, testing each at several different speeds, to see what was making the sound. Finding no possible candidates, we began to wonder what else it might be.

We had talked about ghosts, and about monsters that only came out at night, living in the cellar, crawling around in the dark, looking for things to eat. We finally concluded that we were safe because they couldn't climb the stairs. But they could certainly reach through the steps, grab an ankle, and pull you through. We never went down the stairs at night.

Mat looked at me, hesitant, pondering the lesser of the two evils—lightning or monsters—until we heard a creaking sound, bark ripping apart, slowly at first, but then gaining momentum as the branch, obviously very heavy, accelerated into its fall.

I waited for the house to shudder, for the roof to cave in, but it wasn't our house that was hit. Mat chose the stairs when the object crashed, a deafening thud that vibrated through our walls, and of glass shattering, followed by a *whoosh*, the branch settling in. I ran to the window.

My flashlight cast only a dim light out into the dark, wet weather, and I had to wait until the next flash of lightning, several minutes, before discovering that the cottonwood tree on the south side of our house had been hit, split in half, by the lightning, and had fallen on our neighbor's roof.

Someone came out with a flashlight, for less than a minute, standing in the rain, and then disappeared back inside. I heard some banging from inside the house, possibly for hanging some kind of cover over a window, and then there was only the storm.

Mat stayed gone. I shined the flashlight down the stairs, and the dim light exposed no bodies, and no blood. I assumed he lived, and figured I'd find out in the morning. I went back to bed, dreaming of lightning, tornadoes, and monsters.

Mat survived. The branch on our neighbor's house was cut up before noon, and the gutter was straightened, but the window still had to be replaced. Their TV antenna also had to be remounted on the roof.

Oddly enough, it was the lightning strike that solved the mystery of the creaking door. While the repairmen were up on our neighbor's roof with their ladders, one of them noticed that our wind vane was having trouble, and offered to adjust and oil the shaft, which he did.

I walked across the street and compared the antennas of our house to those of our neighbors. Within a few feet, they were all about the same, and the cottonwood, the part still standing, was not as tall as our antenna. The branch had broken at a fork in the trunk, with the larger side falling off, so I figured it would have been taller than the part still standing by at least six feet, which would have put it up slightly higher than the antennas.

I wandered over to our TV antenna wire and investigated the place where it disappeared into the house, and noticed a second wire also coming down from the roof, following the gutter along the corner, and going to a metal stake in the ground. Next door, Mitch appeared on his front porch.

"Mitch," I said. "Can I ask a question?"

"Ask all you want," said Mitch. "Don't know I can answer."

"What's this wire for?"

"That?" said Mitch, crossing the lawn to join me. "It's a ground wire."

"What's it for?"

"If lightning strikes, it's supposed to go down this wire instead."

"Why?"

"Looking for ground, I suppose. Didn't work at my house though. I forgot to unplug the TV, sounded like a bomb went off. We were all in bed so nobody got hurt."

"Your TV exploded?"

"Yep. That's why I'm late for work, had to clean up the glass."

"But you had a ground wire?"

"Well, yeah. I just forgot to unplug the TV."

"So . . . it went into the house instead of going down that wire?"

"Yeah, but . . . "

We both started in the direction of his antenna wire, located on the other side of his house. I wanted to see what kind of damage had been done, and I think Mitch wanted to confirm that he actually had a ground wire.

I was speculating that the first strike, the one that woke up Mat and I, was the one that took out Mitch's TV. Minutes later, another strike hit the tree on the other side of our house. Why not our antenna?

What had spared us? Was there more to this religion thing than met the eye? Were there advantages to Grandma being a Sunday school teacher? I wondered if perhaps I wasn't taking her lessons seriously enough.

Mitch and I discovered that the ground wire had been disconnected from the stake, and was coiled up and dangling at about the same place where the signal wire entered the house. Lightning chose the TV path instead, and had a clean shot inside.

"Well, I'll be," said Mitch. "Disconnected when they painted the house!"

"The painters did that?"

"I told 'em OK, as long as it was *reattached*," said Mitch, turning and heading for his front door. "They owe me a TV!"

The way I figured it, it was possible that our house got hit, but that the ground wire had worked, and Grandma had unplugged the TV. All things were done right. Armed with this knowledge about ground wires, I got on my bike and headed out to pay Crazy Eddie a visit.

sunflower

Mike Rancourt

that was the summer we folded our hands
before dinner, picked corn from our teeth
for hours, tonguing till morning. at breakfast
i couldn't go on, and spoke little, pushed potatoes
around my plate—*screeks* till you moved your hand
to my wrist. one intimate moment drowned
in my nostrils, in a vinegar-gag of condiments, cleansers.
that was the breakfast i folded your hand
before leaving, the dishes smeared with ketchup,
circles of sunflower oil and salt.
i've always imagined those dishes crashing
the door as i left, shattered triangles and wedges,
steeple-shaped porcelain, powdered at the edges,
swept in a dustpan, ketchup and oil and salt
on the foxtail's bristles. i've always imagined
your hands in the gloves you wore for spring cleaning.
the powdery itching, the burning and swelling
that fall in the kitchen of unfolding hands.

The Rush

Veronica Andrew

The rush is on, a poet once said
long ago, but it is still happening

and I will witness it
with my paper and fingers,
a husbandry in hasty ink.

The rush is on, outside.
The parade ended days ago
but its hues worked their way into the trees
and now ripen like fruit.
A yellow worm severs a stem
with its puckered teeth,
rides a leaf to the ground.
Birds report to each other:
The rush is on.

The rush is on, all around. Look there,
a young boy sits on a bench
reading about Benjamin Franklin.
The rush is on for him, and for Ben, too,
scratching with his feather,
knotting a string, listening to rain
outside his colonial windows.
He knows it will come: a day
when blood meanders across dirt roads
and men speak his words
while lifting their knives to the sun.

The rush is on, as it always was.
We've peered into your backyard,
found the Garden of Eden.
Quickly, tug that carrot up
by its ferny plume—
this time we'll begin our era
with a root.

The Moon Daughter

Zoe Ghahremani

— Chapter 1 —

The first time Rana held her newborn, she did exactly what she had done with her other two children: she reached for the tiny fist and gently peeled back the fingers. Counting all ten digits, she took a deep breath and exhaled. With the room being so cold, Rana decided she'd count the toes later when the baby's feet were exposed.

Like most Iranian women in the sixties, Rana had planned to deliver her baby in a hospital with her doctor present. But the first contractions had come late at night while her husband was out again. With no taxis and not even a carriage in sight, getting around in Shiraz's unforeseen snow would have been impossible. She was grateful the servants had found anyone at all.

The midwife, a stranger to Rana, seemed frantic and acted as though she blamed her patient for the way things had turned out. "Such a head on a baby," she said, "let alone for someone with *your* small frame." The woman wiped her forehead on the sleeve of her uniform. "Mrs. Erfan, I'm afraid your tear is too irregular to stitch." And she hurried about, muttering more indistinct words that had the sound of frustration.

Rana closed her eyes and tried to mask her anxiety. After a moment of absolute silence, she felt a towel being pushed between her thighs.

"Hold that tight," the midwife commanded. She took Rana's hand and placed it on her abdomen over the area of the worst cramps. "Press hard here. That should help to stop the bleeding." Then, as if having sensed how cold Rana felt, she pulled the bedcovers up and tucked them around her.

Rana heard water splashing, followed by the infant's cry, now softer than the previous loud wails. Before she had a chance to look, the cries turned to a soft murmur and soon faded into the next room. She smelled burning wild rue and knew it to be her old nanny's attempt at wishing good health for mother and child. The smoke now mixed with the odor of fresh blood and iodine vapors made the air too heavy to breathe. Following hours of labor, Rana felt woozy and the pain that shot through her made it hard to focus on the midwife's instructions. Muffled voices outside her door sounded as if people were talking under water. Rana welcomed the cold draft as someone opened the door and she heard Dayeh's voice.

"Congratulations, Major Erfan. You have another little lady."

Rana perked her ears, unable to predict her husband's reaction to the news of a third daughter. There was a long pause.

"How surprising!" His response sounded more like a grunt.

Dayeh chuckled as if it had been a joke. "God's gift, Sir, and what a beauty at that."

Another silence.

"*Ahmad,*" Rana tried his name, but her lips felt too dry and her voice wouldn't come out. What was there to say to him anyway? She held the bedcovers in clenched fists, listened and hoped, but soon heard the hammer of his heavy boots fading down the marble hallway. Somewhere in the distance a door slammed, and nearby, women whispered.

Rana wondered if the energy that drained from her and the emptiness it left behind could be what it felt like when the soul left a body. As her mind filled with images of her children, her grip loosened, allowing her hand to slip away. Weightless, she felt herself being pulled into shadows and sank deeper and deeper into a dark well.

The warmth that caressed her face carried the promise of a bright sun and circles of light moved inside Rana's eyelids like fireflies. Keeping her eyes closed, she tried to pull herself up to a sitting position.

"Oh, *khanoom* is up!" The young girl, Banu, had more ring to her voice than Rana's headache could tolerate.

"Please close the drapes," Rana pleaded.

The hooks jingled as they slid on the metal pole.

Rana opened her eyes and squinted at the remaining light. "Where's my baby?" she asked, conscious of the silence around her.

"She's with Dayeh, ma'am."

"Can't believe I slept the entire night."

A wide-eyed Banu shook her head. "Oh, you slept most of the day, too, ma'am. You must be starved."

Rana shook her head. "Not really."

"Dayeh has prepared a special meal. You'll need your nourishment."

Rana nodded with some reluctance. Nourishment. Had anyone fed her baby, and if so, what kind of milk had they given her? Banu was gone before Rana had a chance to ask more questions. And where were the girls? Marjan could be at school, but what about little Vida, who didn't like going anywhere without Mommy?

Banu returned, pushing the door with an elbow and carrying a large tray.

"How *is* the baby?" Rana asked.

"Oh, beautiful as the moon she is," Banu said setting the tray on the nightstand. "Such thick eyelashes on a baby? *Mashallah,* I must burn more incense for her."

Rana touched her deflated tummy and felt as if all the weight missing from her middle had gone to her sore breasts.

"Has Major Erfan returned?" Rana hoped her anxiety wouldn't show.

"Not yet," Banu said while straightening the bedcovers to secure the tray. "He called earlier. I heard Dayeh tell him you were resting."

He stayed out all night?

Rana surveyed the food: Hot bread, soft-boiled eggs, and a bowl of *kachi*—the saffron pudding her old nanny thought a must for a new mother's strength. Rana took a spoonful, but the smell of rosewater made her feel sick again. She swallowed with difficulty and pushed the tray away.

"Take this, dear, and just bring me some water."

Moments later, Dayeh strolled in without bothering to knock. She carried the baby wrapped in a floral blanket and presented her with such pride as if she herself had a part in her creation. She chanted in her shaky old voice, "I have a daughter, *shah*—the king—doesn't have, she has a face *mah*—the moon—doesn't have!"

With newfound energy, Rana stretched out both arms to receive the infant and placed her own cheek on the warmth of the tiny head. When the initial thrill had passed, she placed the baby on the bed and studied her features, now less swollen and more defined. It was time to absorb the details and familiarize herself with her newest daughter: soft cheeks, flared nostrils, and that tiny button on the upper lip. She leaned closer and inhaled. Oh, how she had missed that milky scent, how she adored her little helpless ones, that soft fuzz of hair, the wrinkled neck. She kissed the top of the baby's head and noticed Dayeh had decorated the baby's gown with all sorts of trinkets: A silver prayer charm in the shape of the holy Koran, a blue glass eye, the word Allah engraved in a silver hand, all joined together with a safety pin and secured on the band that held the baby's swaddling clothes together. When it came to keeping the evil eye away, Dayeh took no chances.

"Pretty little thing, isn't she?" the nanny said and squinted. "I think she resembles you. Sure looks nothing like *them*."

Rana smiled. The old nanny made no secret of her hostilities toward Major Erfan and his entire family, and the only reason Rana tolerated such insults was that Dayeh had practically been a mother to her.

"You got a name?" the nanny asked.

Rana shook her head.

"Well, you better come up with something or she'll grow to be an old woman called Baby." She cackled at her own joke.

"I'll leave that choice to her father."

Dayeh turned her back. "As if *he* cares."

"*Dayeh*! Of course he cares. He just needs time to adjust."

The old nanny busied herself with the curtains, folding the pleats one by one and she tied the stack with a silk cord. "Sounds like you've forgiven that man already."

Rana lay back and closed her eyes. *Forgive?* Her old nanny couldn't be further from the truth. Which of his treacheries was she supposed to forgive? Women absolved their men for infidelity all the time, but how big would her heart need to be before she could forgive him for taking a second wife? The thought was like a fire within, flames that no amount of sighs, or tears, could smother. She wasn't ready to discuss this openly, not even with Dayeh. After all, the nanny was an employee and Rana's husband the head of this family. Besides, Rana did not wish to add more to a subject that had already become the talk around town.

The baby cried and Dayeh rushed over, picked her up and started to pace. "I don't know what goes on inside that pretty head of yours, child, but I don't like the way you put up with your husband's absences."

Rana swallowed hard and wished she could go back to a deep sleep, one that she would not awaken from for days. She could not recall being so weak with her other two, or ever, for that matter. Conscious of the silence around her, she asked, "Where are the girls?"

Dayeh continued to pace while rocking the baby. "At their aunt's. The Major sent them over to his sister's while you were asleep and said they're to stay there for a few days."

Rana wondered how the girls coped with Badri's house full of boys and hoped the cousins got along now that they were guests.

The baby continued to fuss.

"I think she needs a change," Dayeh said, sniffing around the baby.

"Could I do that?" Rana said with enthusiasm.

Her nanny stopped pacing and her worried eyes stared at her. "I don't think you're strong enough. It'll only take me—"

"Please?"

Dayeh nodded and returned the baby with reluctance. "Watch her while I get clean diapers."

Rana put the baby on the bed and smiled at the swaddling clothes Dayeh had designed. Wrapped in multiple layers of cloth from the waist down, the bundle was secured with an embroidered band wrapped all around, making the baby look like a mummy. Rana loosened the band and one by one, unraveled the damp layers. Wrapped too tight, the folds of fabric had left pink lines on the baby's skin. "No wonder you were so unhappy," Rana said, caressing the baby's ankle.

The baby cooed, her tiny legs kicking the air.

Rana stared at the little girl's nudity. "Ah, what would it have taken God to put a little appendage between your legs and end my problem?"

Just then, Dayeh returned and took over. She removed the wet diapers and spread new layers of clean cloth under the baby. After wiping her, she dusted the baby with so much talcum powder it made her cough. Rana held the tiny feet and lifted the infant's legs so the back could also be powdered. As she stretched them down again, she let go with such a start as if she'd been electrocuted.

"Oh, my . . . " she whispered.

"Let me do this," Dayeh said, her sad voice indicating she knew.

Unable to respond, Rana held the tiny legs again and pulled them down side-by-side while staring at the baby's right foot. Noticeably shorter, its toes barely reached the left ankle. Rana let go again and covered her mouth with both hands, unable to breathe. Feeling Dayeh's arm around her, she buried her face into her old nanny's shoulder.

"The midwife gave her to me so quickly, I'm sure she didn't notice," Dayeh said, as if this small fact would change everything. When Rana failed to respond, she added, "I haven't told a soul." She put a hand under Rana's chin, turned her face up, and staring into her eyes, cautioned, "And neither should you."

Rana turned her face. "Oh my God," she whispered and her words had the sound of a deep sigh.

She felt Dayeh's calloused hand rub her neck and shoulder the way it had many times before and her voice poured out her blind devotion. "God will help to even them out as she grows."

Rana drew back. "Oh, will He?" she said and the tears that had gathered for some time now found her cheeks. "Did you stop to think just who created her this way?" Her voice broke amid sobs. "Is this because I'm not religious or is it some kind of sick test?" She looked at the ceiling as if God would be somewhere on the roof, eavesdropping. "It wasn't bad enough to give me another girl, this one had to be crippled, too?"

"Please, child, stop your blasphemy!" Dayeh said.

"Oh, I see, so He won't turn his back on me, but hasn't He already?"

Dayeh whispered prayers of forgiveness, wrapped the diapers loosely around the baby and lifted her.

Before she had turned to leave, Rana reached over and pulled the prayer seal off the baby's clothes. "You won't be needing *that*, my love," she cried out. "God wasn't there when you were conceived, He wasn't there when you took form, and He sure as hell won't be around to help you with that leg."

The baby started to cry again and Dayeh rushed out without bothering to close the door.

For a long while Rana clutched the prayer seal in her fist, thought of her bleak future and wept in silence. She heard Dayeh's sad lullaby in the hallway and watched her nanny's shadow on the wall outside her door, rocking the baby back and forth, back and forth.

With darkness all around her, Rana wasn't sure if it had been the sound of a car that woke her. Extending her arm, she touched the empty space beside her before the door squeaked open.

"Ahmad?" her sleepy voice called his name, but in the light that spilled in from the hallway, she recognized Dayeh's plump outline.

"It's me, child, checking if you're up. It's feeding time. I'll go wake the baby."

"No, Dayeh, please don't. You could bring her to me when she's awake." Before Dayeh had left she added, "Did I hear the Major's car?"

The old nanny seemed to hesitate. "You did. It's turned out to be a cold night and he came for his overcoat." She paused before adding, "But he's gone again."

Grateful for the darkness, Rana kept her poise and acted as if she had no idea where her husband might be going. Somewhere, a woman with no face awaited him. Rana would have to deal with that at some point, but not tonight, not while she lacked the energy to plan a future.

"I'll be back soon, then," Dayeh said and closed the door.

The words Rana had once heard from her sister-in-law now came back. "A true lady learns to adjust." Unsure of how much more adjusting she could handle, Rana sat up and leaned against the headboard. Just then, she heard the car again, now from farther away. She left her bed and, without turning on the light, went to the window. Tiny crystals frosted the windowpane. A pale moon painted the snow blue, giving the trees oversized shadows. Moments later the taillights of the army Jeep spilled red over the driveway. Rana felt a chill as the car disappeared behind the gate and the world around her turned colder.

She knew then the name she would give her daughter, the name of the darkest, coldest, and longest night.

Yalda.

Line Dancing at the Cadillac Ranch

Lisa Hemminger

Wait:
syn . . . copate! Bouncing Jacks, Daniels'
eyes, turning in the ugly man, attached
like a planet to a hot woman in orbit.

Friday night tight jean parade
floorboards vibrant with clomps.
A wave of legs moves flock along
the skim of alligator skin boots, oh

wheels on the floor, too, everyone pivot in
tight Spirograph turns, a hundred fingers point
to one place in the air. You a wild country, I

wander over, drunken bird—heart open, red ink in a bowl.
I nod loosely to a stuffy guy hefting a Stetson.
Ow, his offensive rhinestone buckle but at least I can feel.
I rest my soaked head,
and an old thought bumps in:

Once a long time ago
I used binoculars at a marionette show.
A tiny couple had waltzed
without flaw . . . until the lens.

Their eyes only flipped from a horsehair brush.
Their four hands touched, but never grabbed joy.

This Bird Chest Holds a Bird's Heart

David Tomas Martinez

On our birch wood bed,
Jess was crying in chirps
when I entered in her underwear.
I didn't look like her—
couldn't fill them the way she did,
or shimmy while putting on my jeans,
the bright embroidery peacocking light.
She's a woman who
knows where the sea goes
without seeing its edge.
The kicking of her feet
make the splayed sheets shake
when she wakes and tests the air.
She loves in secret with her socks.
In her intricate answers:
Beauty is never simple.
Beauty is always there.
I wear her underwear to hear her laugh,
a little red bow on the butt to forget death,
to fill our little room without a closet,
painted yellow and filled with holes
from a constant rotation of paintings.
To fill it full of us, full of her eyes
and my arms, full of our mothers—young,
laughing at their six-year-old flapping
in heels, staggering in foolishness.

Elevator Music

Erik Kiviat

The guy standing next to me in the elevator was fat, and I mean really fat. I'm thinking what do you have to do to get that fat? I mean what do you have to eat? I smelled onions somewhere and thought that maybe this guy had a big soggy hero sandwich wrapped in foil under his winter coat and sweater and that it was leaking and reeking. He was disgusting and I began to hate him. He was probably a moron, too, a moron with a big overstuffed hero sandwich that he had been towing along under his coat. I imagined the sight of a huge inflatable kangaroo with an Italian hero sandwich in its pouch where the baby should be. I was wondering, if it got hungry enough, would the kangaroo reach into its pouch and take a bite of the sandwich or the baby. It's a fucking freezing winter day and I'm stuck in this fucking elevator jammed to the doors and rails with every kind of melting pot loser they let in this country. The elevator stopped when Jumbo got on. How lucky can I get?

At least my neck is cushioned. The broad behind me must be real short because her rockets are launching into my neck. I think she's showing off because the pressure increases and then decreases in a slow waltz rhythm. I can't turn around to see if she's a toothless Russian grandma or a fabulous "I took a wrong turn in life" exotic dancer on her way to a 42nd Street peep show palace. In my mind, I've opted for Dreamgirl Dancer in the fifth, not the Chernoble survivor with a thermos of hot borscht.

There's an alarm bell ringing somewhere in the background. Here comes the claustrophobia. All the other toads on this rig are starting to fidget and a kid is crying, no, whining, not yet crying. I can see him when I look up into that round curved mirror in the right-hand corner of the elevator. I can't turn around, but I can see that he has a cast on his arm. It must be new because it's white. His mamacita flings out some Spanish to the kid and he really begins to let it out. The Spanish dagger flies again and the kid stops cold. I wonder what she threatened. Maybe it was, "If you don't shut up Daddy will break the other one." No, I'm thinking Daddy wouldn't be able to do that because he's in jail, so it must be the boyfriend.

Some groping forearm is reaching around from behind to push the elevator alarm button again, but a hanging coat cuff catches on the push-arm of my wheelchair. Oops, caught another one! This one's so stupid it keeps trying to push forward even when hooked. How impolite. I wish I could turn around. Coat Cuff finally gives up and pulls backward but can't unhitch. No "Excuse me or I'm sorry" for rattling my wheelchair cage, just a huge sigh and a curse some where behind me. My feet, if I had any, would be right up against the brushed stainless steel doors of this hospital elevator. Hey, think of it this way—I'll get out first when we finally get going. The metal loins and rubber lips of this can will spread open and I will roll out into the corridor "toots suite" followed by Dream Dancer, Spanish Fly and her offspring and the group of sickly urban hopping toads and Jumbo. Wait, maybe Jumbo will figure the elevator would be a nice place for lunch and he'll just start unpeeling that sandwich.

I think, however, the onionic atmosphere of the elevator might set off toxic waste and biohazard sensors. Hospitals have those things, I know. That would lock down the cab between floors until the men in plastic suits and breathing apparatus come to check it out. It would probably even make the news: "Biohazard crew clears Creedmore Hospital of contamination threat when onion-like fumes seep out of elevator shaft.

"When the elevator is finally entered, however, the team finds a large man in fetal position dead on the floor with half a hero sandwich stuffed down his throat. Fumes are later analyzed and found to be oxidizing Bermuda onion and no foul play is suspected in the shabbily dressed man's demise. It is reported as an incident of M. Cass ham sandwich choking syndrome. The crusty bread cylinder was pulled from the man's throat but it was too late. However a receipt for the thing was found in his pocket and we know that the hero came from Guiglio's Deli on 29th Street and that it was the 'Vesuvio Special' with the works. None of the ingredients alone is considered dangerous but all together, on Italian bread, when stuffed down a moron's throat with sufficient force and anticipation, it could happen."

Well, that didn't happen and we're still in the elevator and it's still not moving. From the back of the elevator comes a cough and then a meek, "Excuse me." Another throat-clearing Mr. Peepers *hmmm* with a little more urgency and another "Excuse me." I'm straining to lift myself a little in my chair to get a different angle on the mirror. I'm thinking just how many sardines and mackerels are packed into this stalled can. I look up at that maintenance diploma they keep on the wall to show how often the Harvard graduate inspectors check out this trap and just how much weight it can carry before it mules down and revolts.

Jumbo pushes it over the edge . . . maybe it's gonna plunge. What floor are we on anyway? If we all take the dive it won't be so bad except they won't be able to dig the graves too quick seeing as how the ground is frozen, and this being the big rotten apple the gravediggers are probably on strike.

Hey, that's strange, the elevator diploma says, "Last inspected February 10th"—that's today—and in fancy lettering, "Maximum occupancy 18 souls." Well, there must be more than eighteen since Jumbo counts for two or three. But doesn't it usually say "Maximum weight 2000 pounds or 18 people"? It says "18 souls." Freaky man, I guess these are my soul mates for the ride.

Hey, anyone got some feet they can spare? Look, over here, "podiacly disassembled," removed, exited from me, room to spare at the bottom. You got 'em, I need 'em. Hey, we got to get moving. I need to roll out of here and get a drink. Screw it. I hate all you brainless, damaged walkers. Big thrill for you, stuck on the Creedmore elevator. Some of you probably consider this a vacation. Want a vacation? Try Vietnam, a thrill a minute. Quang, Dang, Bang Bang, down we go, off they come, never to be seen again.

The lights are out. There's no sound. This is really going to freak this tribe out. Surprise, surprise, they're all quiet, even the kid. Now there's a light beam, a squint of a light bouncing off the round mirror up top. The laser beam is hitting off the curved mirror right into my goddamn eyes like a bank shot off the rail into the side pocket. Where's that coming from? Someone got a flashlight? I can't turn around in this chair. Hey, can you get that light out of my eyes? *Por favor, 'Cita, no luz, no lumier.* Hey, you guys all frozen? Rat got your tongue? Hey kid, who's your Daddy? Kill that beam or I'll—

Rodney?

What?

Rodney and his wheelchair did a fast 180 turnaround, the tires leaving a black rubber snow angel on the elevator floor. Someone strong, very strong grabbed the pull bars of his chair and whipped him around in place.

Rodney was dizzy and he shook his head and blinked before he took in the fact that the elevator was totally empty. There were now doors on the other side of the cab, the side he was facing. He was pretty sure they weren't there before, but it was crowded when he got on, maybe he didn't get a good view, but where were Jumbo, the kid, Mamacita, and the other fish? Where were all the losers?

OK, it's the meds they give me, the meds. I must have blacked out and they all got off except me. This sardine can must be working again. It's just like those dogs and cats and rats to leave me here.

How about some nice Muzak from that speaker up near the mirror? Some nice soothing elevator music to calm me down while the meds wear off, then I'm outta here.

Instead a voice comes clearly through the speaker. It's a strong voice.

"They were all dead Rodney. They all died in this hospital. They all made trips in this same elevator before, from emergency room to the morgue—heart attacks, accidents, murders, suicide. These are your soul mates. They came in the front door and went out the back door. They volunteered to take time out and escort you. Isn't that nice Rodney?"

"You mean ghosts?" Rodney answered, not even questioning the voice or why it existed or how bizarre and crazy this moment in the elevator was. It was as though an unexpected friend had arrived and instead of being shocked and surprised you would say, "Hello Al, haven't seen you in thirty years. Take care, gotta go. By the way, are you dead or alive."

"Rodney, get out of the chair. We have to go."

He couldn't stand up since the Quang Dang Bang Bang copter gig in Nam.

No feet.

"I can't. Are you crazy? Who are you?"

"I'm The Dreamer. Stand up Rodney."

Rodney pushed himself up out of the wheelchair. He knew he was standing but he didn't know how and he wouldn't look down. If he did he would have noticed that he was floating as the double doors on the wrong side of the elevator opened. Nice calming elevator music began to play and Rodney heard the voice say in more gentle tones, "Come on Rodney, it's time."

"Son of a bitch," Rodney thought as he clenched his fists and fell back hard into his chair. "Thorazine, voiceman, that's my dreamer, you son of a bitch. Thorazine calms the mind, starts the all-day elevator music in the head. I can play it and dream anytime I want without you ghostman, and right now I'm dreaming these fat and ugly lowlifes are gone, and they are, and I'm dreaming."

The elevator doors opened and Rodney faced a crowd of newcomers in the corridor all ready to push their way onto the elevator.

New soul mates huh, Rodney thought, as he steeled himself to take charge of his unit and make his way out into the cold corridor alone with rifle pointed into the brush and double-bubble clenched into a toothy tank tread pattern between his upper and lower jaw.

"Make way for me, Losers. I'm coming out and I don't care if I die if I take you Gooks with me."

Rodney gripped the wheels of his chair with his gloved hands, the leather biker gloves with all the fingers showing. Those gloves offer no protection if you go down and scrape across the pavement. You'll lose all the fingertips first then the flesh on your palms is dragged and skinned off, but you go down macho. Only fags wear helmets and ride Jap bikes. If you go down in a Quang Dang Bang Bang chopper, the kind that gets shot down by Gook fire, you can lose all your buddies, and some parts already mentioned and one or two not mentioned in polite society. Thorazine, Demoral, these take care of you. Instant elevator music, my man. For fatboy Jumbo it's a stinking sweaty under-the-coat-on-a-winter-day hero sandwich. I do hope you choke, my man. I do hope you choke and die. What the hell did you ever do to deserve to live?

Rodney gripped the wheels and lowered his head to push his way out into the corridor and through the crowd, but all the people simply walked right through him and into the elevator cab. Rodney started shooting. He was surrounded and fired in every direction, up into the trees, down into the brush, straight up into the ceiling of the elevator. He spun around and fired continuously in a 360-degree circle, waist-high, the bullets punching holes in the metal walls of the elevator cab at a consistent height—two feet, eight inches above ground. He mowed down all eighteen passengers, all the enemy, all Gooks all dead now like they should be.

Rodney was smart, he peeked up into that little curved mirror and spotted some movement. It was from somewhere in the back, under the bodies. He turned again and sprayed the pile with an umbrella of rounds. He reached for a grenade on his belt, but felt only his flannel shirt, sweat pants and khaki parka. The dirty gray sweats were tied at the bottoms with rope, at the ankles.

Elevator music, it plays in a steel box that goes up and down ten hundred thousand times. It plays in the steel box of your head to keep you safe. It's all programmed to keep you in your zone and out of the alone zone.

Sometimes we don't even notice that it's playing at all. We are ghosts crowded together ever so close, but when the music—the right music—is playing we have an excuse that we desperately need to survive until the end of the ride, and we can't wait for the end of the ride when we don't have to look into each other's eyes and hear what we are all saying and feel what we are all suffering. For just enough time, we can hold our breath and stare up to where the music is coming from or close our eyes even tighter and let peaceful illusion take over.

Maybe it's love. Maybe it's Thorazine, maybe it's fear, maybe it's fitful sleep hoping for deep sleep and pulling the covers over and hoping it will all go away. We hear the music, and there are so many tunes, an infinite selection of human Muzak to ban the silence and to provide a rose-petal covered trampoline to soften our fall when we see the jungle coming up faster and faster as we spin around uncontrollably.

The guys in the morgue tied the identification toe tag to his left thumb, lacking the convenience of toes.

I Am Shomer

Allison Wright

I said I wanted to bathe her
She had departed but her journey had been arduous
If you had asked her, she would have said
Jesus didn't have such a hard time
I understood what she meant
Jesus was willing, she was not

I lifted her up
Like Gaia, guiding her to my breast
Her weight fell into me
And I held her as she had held me long ago

Her skin was damp with scent
The shroud of decency covering her dark with sweat
I peeled it off, like a snake shedding its skin
Gently, all in one piece, careful of the eye caps

I laid her down exposing the ravages left behind
Her expression taut, a facelift gone too far
The planes of her cheeks rising like endless hills
Only to fall into darkness where the path to her soul
        had been

I bathed her with cucumber and melon
Warm water cascading against the tide
Her skin, thin, worn, speckled like a robin's egg
Bones jutting into air, the New York skyline

Slathered in cream, I placed my hands upon her
Moving freely across the landscape of her body
Giving her in death
That which she could not give herself in life

My knees bent against the earth
My head held in honor
A lifetime of gratitude
Reborn as her pagan Shomer

My Father's Gift

Stephen McDonald

A pale memory of moon rested low in the sky
when he rose from the room he shared

with my mother to enter mine, soft white
hands brushing my shoulder, awakening me

for morning Mass, then teaching me to tie
the knot at my neck his father had taught

him to tie. He led me into the dark hallway,
fingers fluttering like a blessing along the black

wrought iron of the balustrade, lifting to touch
the picture of Jesus at the top of the stairs.

In the yard we passed the liquidambar rising
in its crosshatch of shadows, tight green buds

swollen with life, the evergreen pear
discarding its gown of white petals one prayer

at a time. Later, candles cast shadows across
stained-glass windows as yet unlit by any hint

of morning. Statues of saints rose like visions
from blue recesses along marbled walls.

I have not forgotten the tug of my father's fingers
that morning as he snugged my tie, nor the way

he dropped to one knee to whisper into my ear
I wish I had been a priest. When he died

in early morning darkness, the anointing oils
still fresh on his pale skin, I wondered

if he knew what his wish had bound me to,
how tightly I was tied to his prayers. In the dark

he had offered to me his one gift, a knot
I would spend the rest of my life tying, untying.

Riding an Indian

J. F. MacDonald

She yearned to be held and he to hold. She could tell one species of salvia from another and could hold her own on a drag strip. He dropped out of school, ran away from a foster home at the age of fourteen, and made then lost $186,000 trading bonds before he was twenty. They walked away together after totaling a stolen Jaguar on Highway 1, south of Ensenada. He held her interest when he told her stories that weren't true. He held her with leather in a room near the beach in San Quintin. He held her together when her grandmother died, the only family she'd known. He held her close for three years then left to climb Everest.

That's what he said but he didn't go to Tibet. He went to London then to Greece with a girl he met in Soho. He was in Greece for a year and a summer with, but not holding, the girl. After the girl left, before he quit mixing drinks at night and walking beaches at noontime, he decided he would go to Tibet. He needed money and a winter to prepare.

He went to New York and traded bonds, stock options, futures, financial instruments. But he could not trade his heart.

In April he bought a Harley and left the city to find her, Miranda. Late May in Tucson he heard that she had gone to San Diego riding an Indian. On a Saturday afternoon in June, he found the Indian parked in gravel outside a wholesale nursery. Sun reflected sky off its blue curves and melted into its riveted leather bicycle seat. It's her, he thought.

He sat on a cart to wait and, when the lot was free of waiting customers, she came to him and said, "I wanted the mountain to get you."

The trowel in her hand was steady but he noticed a twitch in a bare knee. He thought of her long blonde hair trailing in the wind and said, "Nice Indian."

"Why did you come back?"

"You," he said. The fronds of a nearby palm fluttered in the breeze, playing their shadows in the space between them. "Is it fast?"

"Faster than you and more reliable."

"Like shit. It won't beat my Harley."

"If it does, will you go away?"

They met on 78 beneath bouldered hills above Escondido. "First one to Ramona," he said and they were off. He passed her doing 110 at the bend before Indian Oaks Road. A truck hauling produce was moving onto the highway, blocking him. His Harley spun and slid under. Sky and asphalt dancing in his vision, the heat of the road through his leathers, the sound of steel and bone, all mixed in a moment with the presence of her in his heart.

Before the sirens, she held him and he asked, his voice faint, "Did I win?" Then he was out. She pleaded, "Please, please, don't go." And she held him, and held him.

Curtain—An Elegy

Sylvia Levinson

All the world's a stage
And all the men and women merely players . . .
　　—William Shakespeare, *As You Like It*, act 2, scene 7

I
The daffodils on my dresser are a week old.
Tight buds when I bought them,
they opened overnight,
and raised their trumpeted throats.
Looking at them, I felt hope.
Now the petals of their lush yellow skirts are
sere, papery-thin; the tops of their green swords
browned, curling over.

II
Once, a fledgling bird fell onto my balcony.
The size of a plum, brown fluff tipped with yellow.
It flapped helplessly for a few minutes
and I felt helpless, too.
Then, like a spent balloon,
it lay stiffening on the gray cement.
I placed it in a lavender gift bag,
among a few red geranium blossoms.
It was not till the next day that I put it in the trash.

III
I'm sitting in the tenth row, orchestra center,
midway through act 1 of an Irish play
and suddenly wonder—what would Philip think of this—
remembering how quick he was to make judgments,
how he gave his opinion out loud during intermission
even if the playwright or director was within earshot.

I gave him bread and salt and purple dishtowels
when he moved into his new apartment.
He once gave me a leather passport case
and a red suede-covered journal.

Erin in black stockings

Billy Hughes

I find Erin, she is nineteen,
living on Del Monte—
she does not grow old.
Not having a real father,
Erin is the one who can redeem you—next
to the photo of a nude Isabella
Rosellini, clippings of lavender
in a drinking glass, band-aids, buttons
collected in a small wooden box.
In the warm room of March, I believe Erin
when she says there's nothing funny about this—
her crossed legs exposing the back of a thigh
bordered by a single shade of black
and an off-white dress. I won't wake with her,
a fact which demands I mention these:
I've kept promises I never made, kept
a list of names of suspect saints,
kept a collection of dandelion seeds,
kept a distance which now can't be closed.

Remembering the '80s

Eber Lambert

I had lunch one rainy afternoon with Oliver North and Mother Teresa. We ate at *Faim du Monde*, an overpriced Ethiopian steakhouse located in southeast Washington D.C. Parking was a problem. So was getting to the door. The local homeless and soon-to-be homeless had coagulated in the entryway, forcing us to hop over the sprawled bodies with their Army-Navy surplus bed rolls and recently issued mental health center release papers. Ollie and I had no problem hopping over them, but Terri doesn't hop. She touched and blessed each one. Near the entrance, Jesse Jackson sat among the squalor in an Armani suit with a sign that read *Free South Africa—End Apartheid*. It seemed a tad ironic to me that the African-Afrikaaners were getting more attention than the African-Washingtonians in the crumbling neighborhoods surrounding us, but I put a C-note in his cup nonetheless and complimented him on his diamond-studded watchband.

Once inside, we were greeted by Ronald Reagan—the maitre d'—standing at a lectern looking a bit dazed, twitching his head like he always did. He hadn't worked there long, had a dickens of a time keeping the table numbers straight and couldn't close out the register if his life—or everyone's, for that matter—depended on it. Yet the trust-fund waitstaff considered him one of the best maitre d's ever. After blubbering out a folksy non sequitur, Ron began to wander aimlessly around the restaurant, and we followed him because—well, because he was just so endearing. He sat us at a booth near the west wall—seemed quiet and cozy enough. Then he told us the soup of the day was a ketchup bisque and suggested a recently acquired El Salvadoran wine—the Four Dead Nun shiraz.

Our waiter, Donald Trump, came to the table in a New York minute. He explained that the day's specials were the Wingless Chicken Chernobyl with a weapons-grade chutney, and a Valdez Kelp and Seafood Salad with blackened mew gull with a forty-weight dressing. Tempting, but we decided to order from the menu. Ollie had the BGH-marinated prime rib—shredded of course—with the Persian couscous and Nicaraguan plantains. It seemed like an odd combination. Terri ordered the wooden bowl of expired Wheatena made with tainted water and a side of flies.

Me, I'm ovo-pesca-avi vegetarian, which basically means I don't eat mammals. I do this for my health. I only eat real stupid animals like birds, fish and members of the crustacean family. Someone once told me being okay with eating chicken but not beef and pork was arbitrary and hypocritical. I told them it was no more arbitrary than eating cow and pig but not dog or cat. You have to draw the line somewhere, and I decided to neatly draw it between class and phylum. So I had the dolphin-safe tuna melt with Velveeta on Wonder bread. And the escargot in garlic and partially hydrogenated palm oil.

After ordering, Terri started a long-winded diatribe about the Vatican's new five-point strategy to increase market share in Asia. She was a nice enough lady, but her speech was ridiculously slow and laborious. Ollie grew increasingly more impatient listening to Terri yammer on while he waited for his meal. He began playing around with his napkin, holding it over the candle and pulling it away before it kindled. Terri finally got annoyed. In a restrained shout, she said she knew G. Gordon Liddy and that he was no fucking G. Gordon Liddy. Then she slapped his hand and told him to cut the shit. That's when the napkin caught on fire.

Donald rushed over to douse the blaze with some PCB-enriched milk from a sterling silver pitcher. Well, this wasteful display set Terri off in a complete rage. She grabbed her dessert fork and jabbed it deep into Donald's thigh. He let out a nasally rich-guy scream and fell back on the table next to us where, of all people, Jane Fonda and Jerry Falwell were engaged in one of their little matinee rendezvous.

They were both pretty loaded. Jane had on a desert camo leotard and yak wool legwarmers, looking a little sleazy in the push-up bra and Khmer Rouge lip gloss. Falwell was in full papal regalia, dressed in a long white satin robe and sporting his Grand Wizard yarmulke. He had just raised his plate up to his mouth to drink the blood red *au jus*—very *gauche* if you ask me—when

Donald flopped on their table with the dessert fork impaled in his thigh. Both Jane and Jerry burst out laughing. Jerry blew the *au jus* out of his nose and all over his angelic white day-cloak. It stained right through to the leisure suit.

That caused Ollie to start cackling, which prompted Terri to turn around and deck him with a single blow between those beady puppy-dog eyes of his. She screamed, "Fuck all you guys!" and stormed out of the restaurant. She was out of control. It reminded me of the time she did too much acid at Nixon's party. Ollie shook it off, climbed back into his chair and started humming "The Star-Spangled Banner," stopping briefly to emphatically deny—to no one in particular—all recollection of the previous five minutes.

Jane suddenly looked a little peaked and stumbled off to the ladies room, counting her steps out loud as she went. Poor Don fell to the floor writhing in pain until Falwell reached down and yanked the fork out of his leg, making sure to give it a good twist first. Michael Dukakis appeared out of nowhere, helped Don up and walked him back to the kitchen, which was filled with Chinese college students on a hunger strike, who all started grabbing at him and kicking him with their Nikes.

This was when I noticed Muammar Gaddafi, Manuel Noriega, and Secretary of State George Schultz sitting together a few tables over. Not wanting to be rude, I went over to say hello and tell them that I never realized that they all had the same face. George reminded me that LBJ, Brezhnev, and Golda Meir did too. Rebuked, I said it was nice to see them talking to each other again. This produced a stony silence. Each of them just sat there frozen, nervously holding his butter knife, not saying a word or making eye contact.

I walked back to my table. Ollie had covertly slipped away, leaving me the check. He always does that. So cloak-and-dagger, those NSA guys. Bill Gates had replaced Don, and came over to the table to ask me if there was anything else I needed. He made me feel a bit rushed. I asked him to put the whole bill on Terri's tab because I was a little short on cash. Everyone always does that. It's what she lives for.

I liberated my jacket from Margaret Thatcher, who was manning coat check. Tipped her forty Argentine pesos even though I was a little weirded out by her flirtatious wink. Outside, the homeless and soon-to-be homeless stood in a line that wrapped around the corner, waiting for free government cheese. Or crack. It's always hard to tell. So I cut through the alley, where I found George Bush One and Saddam Hussein in yellow hazmat suits loading canisters of mustard gas and anthrax into a Ford Aerostar. A few yards away Malcolm Forbes, dressed like a member of the mujahideen, held a ladder for Mikhail Gorbachev, who had propped it against a wall evidently built years ago to create a foreshortened dead end out of the already blind alley. Gorby was scrubbing off the Polish graffiti while a group of German tourists trapped on the other side chipped away at the wall with picks and sledgehammers as they sang Pink Floyd's "Another Brick in the Wall." The harmony needed work.

When they finished loading the van, Bush knocked on a nearby service door and Willie Horton emerged. He crawled into the van's driver's seat while Malcolm, Gorby, Saddam, and George jumped in the back. Willie gunned the engine and the vehicle sped away.

I just stood there as the acid rain turned to a basic drizzle, listening to the sirens and AK-47s off in the distance and wondering what the '90s could possibly have in store for us.

Palinode

Brian Hayter

Gepetto makes a boy into a puppet.
Says: I'm tired of fixing the boy's lunches

and picking his shit up off the floor—
only to get disrespected, suffer the boy's lies.

He hangs the puppet by the strings
next to a lion puppet and a bear puppet.

He says: this will be a much nicer arrangement for us.
The next day he takes the puppet down

at lunch time and sits him at the table like a real boy.
"You haven't touched your porridge,"

but the wooden eyes drill straight through Gepetto.
Mothers at the park will stare

when Gepetto puts the puppet on the swings
and pushes him back and forth, back and forth.

One of the other boys makes fun of the puppet
and Gepetto smacks him across the face.

Gepetto goes home and cuts his own arm with a razor
and is weeping. "I am such a weak man, so weak."

He drinks a scotch, rests the puppet on the workbench,
and places the spoon against the wooden lips.

For Christ's sake, he says, eat something.

Uzurazuki (The Month of Quail)

Jeannine Hall Gailey

Wednesday I tried to lie down but couldn't sleep. Outside it was daylight, I'd forgotten my name and who I was. A quail kept calling, one quail all alone, outside my window. Was he waiting for me? I knew what day of the week it was, what outfit I was wearing, but memory is like that sometimes, water, it slips through. A quail crying alone for six days. I wish I knew where we were going, this quail and I. Whether I was going to leap through the window into some other life. Whether or not I would wake up one day and suddenly know flight. Follow the clouds away from here, the fever, the heat. Follow some dream I can't remember.

What did you say?
The name of the rocks here,
not granite, not limestone.

Something more blue. Agate? The way you said my name sounded like wings. Maybe I do have wings. What to remember, the way I made that sound like crying, the taste of rust rising in my throat like wings.

On Seeing Peter for the Last Time

Josie Rodriguez

I've traveled this road many times before—Highway 15 to 395, north through Owens Valley filled with daisies like cups of sunlight in the spring. The Eastern Sierra mountains topped with snow peaks looked like tufts of cotton candy as the sun dipped behind the mountains.

I've traveled this road before—with my husband and three sons—small squealing children ready to camp where Uncle Peter was the park ranger at places like Lone Pine, Mount Whitney, Mammoth Mountain. There were memories of hiking, listening to stories and watching shooting stars overhead around a campfire after a canned spaghetti dinner and S'mores for dessert. Peter told our kids that they could be honorary park rangers if they would help him clean the bathrooms. They enthusiastically did the job as Pete pinned an official-looking park ranger badge on each of them. Peter helped us get prime camping spots and let us know when the ponds would be stocked with trout. And the porcupine that Peter cared for near his home in Mammoth was the hit of that summer.

I've traveled this road before—where on a cold November afternoon with snow at their feet, Peter and Joan made their vows to love and honor each other "until death do us part," as family and friends toasted them with joyful hearts.

I've traveled this road before—on our way back from Lake Tahoe through Bishop. A promise of barbequed tri-tip and red wine gave me the needed incentive to hike all the way to Gem Lake with my brother and his wife, ending with stories and laughter shared in their kitchen in Aspendell.

I've traveled this road twice before—driving Peter home from San Diego after his release from the hospital and devastating surgeries and chemotherapy treatments. Pete could hardly wait to be greeted by his wife and dog, Abby, and to sit in his favorite chair by the big window watching their mountain change with the seasons.

I've traveled this road before but never this journey, never the path we took as we traveled in darkness along stretches of high desert with my mom sitting next to me—moments filled with quiet talk and tears on our way to see Peter for the last time. The entire family was coming to see him—each traveling a different road—at various times—to tell Peter of the love and admiration we had for his incredible courage and grace through nine years of fighting the cancer he called a monster.

As I traveled this road to see my youngest brother and his wife it was so dark that I couldn't see what was outside the window—much like I felt inside as I wondered, Will he be gone by the time we arrive? Did he know of our love and the support we would give to his wife? What would I say? What would I do?

Peter had traveled this road many times before but never this journey where he said goodbye to each of us and took his last breath in the early morning—his wife and his sister, Mary, holding him close.

Our family traveled that road one last time to help ease Peter into heaven, where lakes overflowed with trout, meadows were filled with purple lupine and aspen trees quaked upon his arrival. And we let him go.

Guidelines

Billie Dee

Sit awhile:
clear your nervous mind.

Let the bird outside the window
sing the tune.

Make a list of your lovers:
then take it outside

and show it off:
attach a red string and fly it as a kite.

CONTRIBUTORS

Sandra Alcosser has published seven books of poetry, including *A Fish To Feed All Hunger* and *Except By Nature*. She is the NEA's first Conservation Poet for the Wildlife Conservation Society and Poets House, New York; Montana's first poet laureate and recipient of the Merriam Award for Distinguished Contribution to Montana Literature. She founded the MFA Program in Creative Writing at San Diego State University, and has directed SDSU's International Writers Summer Program at National University of Ireland. She is, or has been, a member of the faculty at the University Michigan, University of Montana, and Pacific University, and a writer-in-residence in Glacier National Park, Yosemite National Park and Central Park, New York. Her poems have appeared in *The New York Times, The New Yorker, The Paris Review, Poetry,* and the *Pushcart Prize Anthology.*

Veronica Andrew grew up in Northern California. She lived in San Diego for seven years and recently completed her MFA at San Diego State University. She now teaches at University of San Francisco. This is her first poetry publication.

Roger Aplon has published eight collections of poetry and one of prose. He occasionally reads his work with musicians from the Trummerflora Collective. He has recently been awarded an arts fellowship from the Helene Wurlitzer Foundation in Taos, New Mexico. You can read and hear examples of his work at: www.rogeraplon.com

Chris Baron began his journey in New York City. Born into the tumultuous life of an artist's family—he survived. He also became equipped for a life of discovery. Naturally, this means he has transformed into a loyal Californian—Chris is passionate about the importance of art as a practical resource for discovering truth—and as a means of survival. Chris completed his MFA in Poetry in 1998, and is a professor at San Diego City College. His work has appeared in a number of anthologies, magazines, and literary journals.

Sydney Brown is the Creative Writing Program Co-Coordinator at Grossmont College, where she teaches poetry and composition. Her fiction and poetry have appeared in *Sonoma Review*, *Southern Anthology*, *two girls review*, *Hawaii Pacific Review*, *red*, *Sunshine/Noir*, *HOW2: Contemporary Innovative Writing Practices by Women,* and *Hunger and Thirst.* Thankful (and quite frankly, a little surprised) for the inspiration domesticity provides, Sydney lives in La Mesa with her husband, Steve, and two schnauzers: Vladimir and Lolita.

D.B. (Donna) Cunningham retired from a career at SAIC to write and travel. In 2008 she published *The Aloha Diary*, a novel set in San Diego and Honolulu. She writes book reviews and articles and is working on her second novel and *People and Places,* a collection of stories.

Former Poet Laureate of the US National Library Service, **Billie Dee** earned her doctorate from the University of California, Irvine. Her work has appeared in numerous anthologies and journals, both online and off. A California native, she lives in San Diego with her partner and a pack of strays.

Judy Geraci is a member of San Diego Writers, Ink, and Thursday Writers at Lestat's. She is currently revising a collection of linked short stories, entitled *Tri-City*. The collection's title story appeared in the 2007 anthology of San Diego Writers, Ink.

Kathleen Elliott Gilroy: Resident of National City for twenty-eight years, resident of Chula Vista for twenty-five years. Retired teacher. Artist, quilter, writes short stories, poetry, is an animal communicator. Active with Feral Cat Coalition. Believes family, friends are important, as is the sacredness of all life. Member of the Laverne Brown Poets group, Oasis poetry group, and a former member of the California Federation of Chaparral Poets.

Zoe Ghahremani is a retired dentist who found true bliss after losing a lifelong battle to the writer within. Following her dream, from Iran to London to Virginia to Chicago to California, she now lives in San Diego, where she can devote her time to the written word.

Jeannine Hall Gailey's first book of poetry, *Becoming the Villainess*, was published by Steel Toe Books. Poems from the book were featured on *The Writer's Almanac* and *Verse Daily*; two were included in 2007's *The Year's Best Fantasy and Horror*. She volunteers with *Crab Creek Review* and teaches in National University's MFA program.

Crystal Hadidian grew up in Austin, Texas and migrated to California for a degree in English at the University of California, Santa Barbara. While there she won first place in the Ina Coolbrith Poetry Contest. She is now at San Diego State University working on an MFA in Creative Writing.

Judy Hamilton is a tax controversy attorney, defending taxpayers against the Internal Revenue Service. She is a third-generation Southern Californian and lives in San Diego on a hill overlooking the bay with her long-time companion Ken and their cat, Kidders. *Small Favors* is her first novel.

Brian Hayter: I have published previously in *Massachusetts Review, Borderlands, Seattle Review, Hayden's Ferry* and others. I have poems forthcoming in *Poetry International, Baltimore Review*, and *Columbia Review*. I am assistant editor at *Spillway Poetry Journal*.

Lisa Hemminger whittled her artistic expressions on Chicago stages as a performance poet and workshop curator. Currently teaching and attending the MFA program at San Diego State University, she is the author of the chapbook collections, *Colossus Taught Us* (Water of Life Press) and *The Complication Compilation* (Loki Graphics).

Peter Hepburn is a full-time caregiver to his disabled brother. A writer of multiple genres, Peter plans to finish his memoir, *Sons of Dead Dads*, by the end of 2009. He contemplates plastic surgery with a goal of looking more like George Clooney and less like Andy Rooney.

Billy Hughes is a native San Diegan. Publication credits include *Pennsylvania English* and *The Surfer's Journal*.

Una Nichols Hynum, a transplanted New Englander, published this year in *Poppyseed Kolache*, and in an upcoming issue of *ONTHEBUS*. In recent years, she was a finalist in James Hearst Poetry Contest, and published in *Margie,* and *The Writer's Digest*.

Eric Johnson teaches English in San Diego. He holds an MFA from the Program for Writers at Warren Wilson College. His poems have appeared in *Atlanta Review*, *The Greensboro Review*, and other journals. His chapbook, *The Exquisite River & Other Poems,* was published by Jeanne Duval Editions in 2006.

Sandra Joss, PhD, is an anthropologist working on a nonfiction book about mixed-heritage, indigenous artists in her home country, Australia. Previously she worked in international development at the World Bank, specializing in Central and South American and Caribbean countries.

Ilya Kaminsky is the author of *Dancing In Odessa* (Tupelo Press, 2004), which won the Whiting Writer's Award, the American Academy of Arts and Letters' Metcalf Award, the Dorset Prize, the Ruth Lilly Fellowship, which is given annually by *Poetry* magazine. *Dancing In Odessa* was also named Best Poetry Book of the Year 2004 by *ForeWord Magazine*. He co-directs San Diego State University's MFA Program in Creative Writing and edits *Poetry International.*

Erik Kiviat is a landscape designer living in San Diego. "My wife Laura and I met in college in New York and served together in the Peace Corps in Morocco. I love creativity and writing. We have always had beautiful Yorkshire Terriers with us."

Steve Kowit's latest collection of poetry is *The First Noble Truth* (U of Tampa Press). He has spent seventy years living among the savages. A teacher at Southwestern College, he advises his students not to join the military.

Eber Lambert grew up in the Peoples Republic of Vermont. Engineer, cynic, father, and unapologetic liberal, he has been writing for thirty years in a futile attempt to stay sane. He recently added a new Roman numeral to his age.

Sylvia Levinson's poetry and prose publications and awards include *Snowy Egret, Blue Arc West, Hunger and Thirst, City Works, Christian Science Monitor, Poetic Matrix, Magee Park,* The Writing Center anthologies, *A Year in Ink, Volume I,* African-American Artists and Writers**,** and *First Friday CD of Year 3*. Her book, *Gateways*, is available at www.sylvialevinson.com.

Lenny Lianne is the author of a full-length book of poems, *A Wilderness of Riches: Voices of the Virginia Colony* (ScriptWorks Press, 2008). She holds a BA in History and an MFA in Creative Writing from George Mason University. She has won awards from the Poetry Society of Virginia and the Wergle Flomp Humor Poetry Contest. She lives in Ramona with her husband.

J.F. MacDonald, trained in physics and an electrical engineer by trade, has participated in San Diego Writers, Ink events since 2006. His First Friday reading, "The Rocking Chair," can be found on *First Friday CD of Year 3*.

Meagan Marshall is a poet and performer from San Diego. Her work has appeared in *The Portland Review* and on *Web Del Sol*. She is currently pursuing an MFA in Creative Writing at San Diego State University.

When not writing bios or sonnets in bathroom stalls, **David Tomas Martinez** lurks along the trolley lines giving hugs to the girls and pounds to the homeboys, all the while remarking how the cigarette butts on the ground look like petals on a wet, black bough.

Stephen McDonald teaches at Palomar College in San Marcos, California. His poetry has been published or is forthcoming in *RATTLE*, *The Crab Creek Review*, *Blue Unicorn*, *The Sow's Ear Poetry Review*, *Passager*, *Pinyon*, and *The Cresset*. His chapbook, *Where There Was No Pattern*, was published by Finishing Line Press in 2007.

The stories "One of These Nights" and "Passing" are excerpts from **Steve Montgomery**'s memoir, *Boy of Steel*, about his experiences growing up as a boy who liked other boys in Mormon-dominated Pocatello, Idaho. Steve's work has been anthologized in *Mourning Sickness* (OmniArts Press), and *A Year in Ink, Volume I*.

Deniz Perin is a writer and translator living in San Diego. Her work has appeared in various literary journals, including *Runes*, *The Atlanta Review*, *Golden Handcuffs*, and *The Raven Chronicles*. Her translation of Ece Temelkuran's *Book of the Edge* is forthcoming by BOA Editions in 2010.

Stephen W. Potts teaches popular culture at University of California, San Diego, where he has won two teaching awards, and children's literature at San Diego State University. Since 1982 he has published books on Joseph Heller and F. Scott Fitzgerald as well as numerous articles, stories, and editorial columns. He edits the online journal *Armageddon Buffet* (www. armageddonbuffet.com).

Michael Rancourt is a graduate of the MFA program in poetry at San Diego State University and a teacher of composition. He is currently at work on an independent project examining divisive political rhetoric of new media and plans to expand the work in the PhD program in Fall 2009.

Dave Riessen studied creative writing at San Diego State University and is a member of San Diego Writers, Ink. He has written two novels, including *You Gotta Have Wings*; several children's stories, including *Kuchan*, published in Japan; and two screenplays. He is a frequent contributor to Dime Stories Open Mic at The Grove in San Diego.

Christine Rikkers is co-editor of *pacificREVIEW*, and editor of *Poetry International*'s New American Poets Chapbook Series. After four years in New York City working in publishing, Christine lived and worked in Nanjing, China, teaching English. She now lives and works in San Diego.

Josie Gable Rodriguez believes that art in many forms is universal toward healing the spirit. A visual artist and writer, she has written essays and poetry since her children were very young. Her book of poems, *Waiting Rooms of the Heart,* was written while she worked in hospital and hospice settings as a clinical chaplain. Her brother, Peter, died during those years; her memoir was written to honor him and to bring healing.

Arthur Salm is former Books editor, feature writer and columnist for the San Diego Union-Tribune.

Kimberly Schultz is a member of San Diego Writers, Ink. She frequently reads at Dime Stories Open Mic in her hometown of San Diego. She'd like to thank JJ Holbert, Ely Rareshide, Midge Raymond, and Linda Salem for their invaluable help with "Terra Incognita."

Carolyn Selman has published poetry and fiction in the UK and had a chapbook published by *Poetry International*. She received her MFA in Creative Writing from San Diego State University and was nominated for Best New Poets 2008. She has read her work at "Celebrating Poetry" in Coronado in 2007 and 2008.

Lizzie Wann has five chapbooks (*Familiars, Naked Wrists, Complicated Skies, 12 Windows, Baseball Poems*), two CD's ("A Wing and A Prayer," "A New Leaf") and various publication credits including *Comstock Review, So Luminous the Wildflowers*, and *Incidental Buildings & Accidental Beauty*. She lives in San Diego.

Pattie Wells is a poet, translator and author of short stories. Her work has been published or will appear in *Green Hills Literary Review*, *Wisconsin Review*, *Sow's Ear Poetry Review*, *Poetry International*, and *ZYZZYVA*. She has taught dance at Grossmont College, Southwestern College, and San Diego State University. Currently, she owns and operates a dance center.

Margo Wilding writes, teaches, and lives in San Diego.

Gary Winters has won numerous awards for short story, poetry, novel, and photojournalism. He was the English editor for a bilingual newspaper in Mexico. Immigration officials severely censured him when he championed Mexican union workers and/ /boys/ /selling chewing gum/ /on the streets of San Felipe. He writes fiction now.

Allison Wright returned to her childhood home in San Diego to care for her elderly mother. Her journey as a caregiver bore witness to her mother's last years of life and gave birth to her voice as a poet. Allison refuses to give up her New York City phone number.

Dolores Young's publications are: Short stories: "On the Road," *Chinese Daily*, New York City (Oct. 25, 1977); "The Seaweed Farmer," AltaMira Press (2002). Poems: *Magee Park Poets Anthology* (2007, 2008), *The San Diego Poetry Annual* (2006, 2007), and *City Works* (2008).

San Diego Writers, Ink is a nonprofit literary organization that nurtures writers and those wishing to explore the craft of writing, fosters a literary community, promotes literature and celebrates artistic diversity.

The Ink Spot, located in the Art Center Lofts, in San Diego's East Village, is our gathering place where we offer classes, groups, workshops, readings, and other literary events. The Ink Spot is also home to the Arts Council Gallery, which features the work of local artists.

SDW, Ink collaborates with other artistic, cultural, and community organizations throughout the city and county to promote literature and to inspire the community of writers.

We are grateful to The Merci Fund at the San Diego Foundation for its generous support, and to Philipp Scholtz Ritterman for his generosity.

San Diego Writers, Ink
P.O. Box 34374
San Diego, CA 92163

The Ink Spot
710 13th St., Studio 210
San Diego, CA 92101

www.sandiegowriters.org

Order additional copies of *A Year In Ink, Volume 1* and *Volume 2* at our website.

www.ingramcontent.com/pod-product-compliance
Lightning Source LLC
Chambersburg PA
CBHW060123260626
47160CB00005B/2000